# The Mystical Love of God

# Also by Peter Falkenberg Brown

*Waking Up Dead and Confused Is a Terrible Thing*
*Stories of Love, Life, Death, and Redemption*

*The True Love Thing to Do:*
*An Interactive Workbook on Finding Love and*
*Preparing for an Enduring Marriage*

**Works in Progress:**

*The Living Compass of Kindness*
*and Compassionate Love:*
*Exploring Love, Beauty, and the Mystical Path*

*The Postmortem Adventures of Edward Wild:*
*The Girl in the Tavern*

*Do You Want to Be Free?*
*Essays on Freedom as the Foundation*
*of a World of Love and Beauty*

# The Mystical Love of God

## Divine Writing Messages from the God Who Is Always with Us

**Peter Falkenberg Brown**

World Community Press
Gray, Maine

*The Mystical Love of God:*
*Divine Writing Messages from the God Who Is Always with Us*
by Peter Falkenberg Brown

© 2021 by Peter Falkenberg Brown

First Paperback Edition

All rights reserved. No part of this book may be reproduced in any form or by any means without permission in writing from the publisher, except for the inclusion of brief quotations in a review.


Published in the United States of America
by the World Community Press
worldcommunitypress.com

This book takes advantage of modern, digital, print-on-demand technologies and may, over time, be printed by more than one printer. If you receive a copy that fails to meet our high expectations of quality, please inform us by emailing:

publishers@worldcommunitypress.com

You may reach the author at peterbrown@worldcommunity.com
if you wish to send him your remarks or feedback about this book.

Cover painting:
"The Soul of the Rose"
by John William Waterhouse, 1908
Oil on canvas, Width: 59.1 cm (23.2 in), Height: 88.3 cm (34.7 in)
Private Collection
By courtesy of Julian Hartnoll/Bridgeman Images

Cover design by the World Community Press and Great Northern Tea
Interior design by the World Community Press

See Image Credits for other image sources.


ISBN: 978-0-9635706-7-3

Publication Date: January 10, 2021

I dedicate this book to my Dear Beloved God, who is, after all, the real author of this book.

# Summary of Contents

Preface .................................................................................... xi
Acknowledgments .................................................................. xiii
A Brief Overview of the Contents of the Book ............................ xv
An Explanation of Terms and Concepts ................................... xvii
Table of Contents of 201 Divine Writing Messages .................... xix

## Introductory Essays by the Author

Searching for the Indwelling God ............................................... 3

Divine Writing Communion and Journeying ............................... 7
  *The Joy of Living with God*

## Divine Writing Messages from the God Who Is Always with Us

## Additional Essays by the Author

My Loyal Friend *(a poem honoring my guardian angel)* ........... 252

Is There A God and What Is God Like? .................................... 255
  *Exploring the Evidence of Love*

The Beautiful Gifts of the Spirit World ..................................... 267

About the Author .................................................................. 289

Image Credits ....................................................................... 297

# Preface

I hesitated for a very long time before I mustered up the courage to publish this book. I'm a curious mixture of shyness and boldness. I have a strong degree of comfort and confidence around people, which allows me to give public speeches, an activity that some people reportedly fear more than death.

The shy part of me kicks in with anything that's deeply private, and one's faith and relationship with God most certainly fits that category. On top of that, the presumption that a person can actually sense or receive words and content from God is controversial. It's ironic because religious people generally approve of anyone's attempt to align their lives with the standards of Godly ethics and directions. People of faith are encouraged to pray and received "guidance" from God. But it's all rather amorphous, and the idea of actually having a real conversation with God and writing down God's words is too outlandish for many.

I truly feel that every person in the world has been created by God to speak and converse with God continuously, and I am confident that no one can be closer to a person than God. Therefore no one is "special" because they can ask God questions and receive the answers and write them down. It just means that they're paying attention to the quiet voice of God within. It's a wonderful process, but it doesn't automatically make you a saint or even a "good person" (at least not right away). But it does mean that your life has the possibility to improve at the soul and heart level, which is the part that really counts the most.

Many people in the world today are experiencing emotional and spiritual suffocation and are starving for a relationship of love with their very own "Dear Beloved." Thus, I offer this book as a service to those who might be inspired by it. The messages were personal, but they also may be valuable to others. So, with that heart and spirit, I offer you, dear reader, this volume of 201 Divine Writing messages from our Dear Beloved God.

I'd love to hear from you with your feedback about the content of this book. If you wish to, you may email me at:

peterbrown@worldcommunity.com

Love and Blessings,

Peter Falkenberg Brown<br>
Gray, Maine

# Acknowledgments

Since this book contains messages that I believe are from God, the first acknowledgment must go to our Divine Source, whom I prefer to address as "Dear Beloved." I am just the scribe.

I also wish to thank Sarah Winslow, a psychic-medium who gave me a one-hour reading on June 16, 2014. After the reading was over, she casually suggested that I might benefit from doing "automatic writing," which often is defined as a process of yielding your hand to a spirit guide who writes content without your intervention. I had tried a variant on that process three years earlier but had abandoned it after a day or two.

Her comment after the reading clicked with me, so that very night, I sat down and embarked on what I prefer to call "Divine Writing Communion," described in the essay of that name. Over the last six and a half years, the spiritual practice of Divine Writing Communion and Journeying has utterly transformed my life. So, thank you, Sarah, for that tiny comment that made such a huge difference to me. You can contact Sarah at sarah-winslow.com.

With all my writing, I give credit to God, with the phrase:

"Deus est auctor amoris et decoris."

("God is the author of love and beauty.")

# A Brief Overview of the Contents of the Book

The 201 Divine Writing messages that I have selected for this book have been arranged chronologically and were received between June 16, 2014, and the end of 2020. The only two that are out of order are the first and the last messages, which I placed in those spots deliberately. You may find it interesting to read the messages in order because they demonstrate growth along a path, but each message is also a stand-alone message of inspiration. They can be read in any order that you prefer.

I've also included four essays that I wrote:

~ Searching for the Indwelling God
~ Divine Writing Communion and Journeying
~ Is There A God, and What Is God Like?
~ The Beautiful Gifts of the Spirit World

The first essay is a glimpse into my own spiritual journey and how I got to the point where I could publish this book. The second explains the process of Divine writing and journeying, the third is an examination of the nature of God, and the fourth reviews what life is reportedly like in the spirit world. All four essays give the divine writing messages a frame of reference. If you have questions about the messages, I recommend that you explore the content in the essays.

# An Explanation of Terms and Concepts

Here is a brief list of terms and concepts that may be unfamiliar.

~ Mysticism: A direct, intimate union of the soul with God.

~ Divine Writing Communion: The activity of asking God questions and then writing down the answers that enter one's mind.

~ Journeying with God: The activity of traveling in the physical or spiritual world with God, either substantially or seen in our mind's eye.

~ The God Prayer: The prayer I created as a variation of the Jesus Prayer of the ancient Christian mystics. It consists of the phrase "Dear Beloved, We Embrace."

~ The Breath of Love Prayer / Meditation / Embrace: This is my practice of reciting the phrase "Dear Beloved, We Embrace" while breathing in on "Dear Beloved" and breathing out on "We Embrace."

Thus, breath can be part of our prayer and meditation, which has a powerful effect.

~ The Jesus Prayer: The phrase "Lord Jesus Christ, Son of God, have mercy on me," prayed by ancient Christian mystics and pilgrims to center one's mind and faith.

~ Golden Bower: This is a phrase that I sometimes use to describe the place where I commune with God in prayer. It's not necessarily a "place" as much as a state of being and mind. But it can also be a place.

~ Seat of consciousness: This was a term that I read in the book *The Untethered Soul* by Michael Singer. It's the soul or higher mind that exists above the pain of daily life, where one can observe one's pain without falling prey to it. From that place, one can say, "I am not my pain."

~ Unio mystica: Mystical union with God; a Christian tradition.

~ Devekut: The Jewish tradition of cleaving to God.

~ Out of body experiences (OBEs): The phenomenon where someone rises out of their body and travels in the astral or spiritual planes, while one's physical body remains alive in the physical world.

~ Near-Death Experiences (NDEs): Similar to an OBE, but precipitated by a brush with death, or sometimes when one is clinically dead, but then recovers.

~ Bilocation: The mystical practice of existing physically in one location while being active and/or appearing in a second location.

~ Flying in the spirit world: Many people have reported that one can fly in the spirit world. Some people experience that in dreams as well.

~ Glemmer / Glemmering: A verb, a neologism. I've had countless dreams in which I experienced sliding down flights of stairs and outdoor steps, with my feet just touching the edges of the steps, as if I were skiing or sliding down the stairs on a shield, as the elf Legolas did in the movie *The Lord of the Rings: The Two Towers*. In my dreams, I got the message that this was called "glemmering." Of course, one cannot do this in real life, but I did it so many times in my dreams (or perhaps the spirit world) that I'm convinced that it is something that one can do in the spirit world. I shall try it out for real, one day.

# Table of Contents of 201 Divine Writing Messages

The God who is always with us ................................................. 13

The flower of love grows with my breath.
It glistens with my tears and my embrace. ............................... 15

Only love will change the world.
Be still and know that I am God. ............................................. 16

How can anyone say that you are not able
to feel my embrace until you are "perfect"? ............................ 17

Embrace me all the time, and
you will be protected against all trials. ..................................... 18

Who is the power that allows you to work?
Who owns the energy that creates you? ................................. 19

What I said to "X" isn't necessarily what I will say to you. .......... 21

I embrace you when you are separated and feel alone. ............. 22

Bring me into every aspect of your life. .................................... 23

My love is so intense that it keeps the universe alive. ............ 25

Embrace me as if your life depended on it—because it does. .... 26

I am with you anyway, whether you
turn from me or not, so don't turn from me. ........................... 27

When you're weak, cry out to me! ............................................ 28

Nothing matches my love. ........................................................ 29

Tell people to follow Me and my essence,
which is my incarnational and mystical love. ........................... 30

You will live with me forever. ................................................... 31

No one can understand how immense I am.
Yet, I breathe together with the smallest creature .................... 32

Your capacity to give love
comes from me—the source of love ......................................... 34

Connect with the reality of my mystical energy of love. ............ 35

Sometimes, you may feel that you have almost
nothing to give. That is exactly when you need Me. ................. 36

You are safe with me ................................................................ 38

What I can't take care of, or do, is do
your part, which is to return my embrace. ................................. 39

Embrace me as you fall asleep; dream with
me; visit with me; travel with me, as you sleep. ....................... 41

By binding your heart to mine, you rise above the fray. ............ 42

You will spend eternity with me,
loving my children and loving my creation. ............................... 43

So what does my face look like?
It looks like all the faces of the universe. ..................................... 45

The intensity of your focus
on being with me will draw you to me. ...................................... 47

Desire is everything, for if there were
no desire, no one would care about anything. ......................... 48

No one can be closer to you than me. ....................................... 49

Cling to me, like David. .......................................................... 51

It all comes down to this—human beings
simply don't feel the immensity of my love for them. ............... 52

A person's capacity to love grows very slowly. ......................... 54

Divine love is unstoppable. ........................................................ 55

The secret is in the intensity of your passionate love for me ...... 56

It's a bower that we carry with us—
it's the atmospheric sphere around us. ...................................... 57

Yes, it is indeed God embracing God. ........................................ 59

Fear cannot be an issue when love is at stake. ........................... 60

Live with me in the eternal now.
Embrace me in the eternal now. ................................................. 61

Some people become spiritually open without love. ................. 62

Every child that finally returns my
embrace brings me an indescribable joy. ................................... 63

The breasts of God .................................................................... 65

Now it is time for you to become
absolutely fastened to me, in a single-minded way. ................... 66

Don't my children need to hear about these things?
They are starving to death, in terms of love. ............................. 67

How does God love every person?
Let me love this person the way that God does. ........................ 68

Easter Sunday: Love is an explosion of joy! ............................... 69

My love takes the long view.
The ten-thousand-year long view. ............................................. 71

Focus on recognizing our union, and
your perception of my presence will grow. ............................... 72

Nothing is stronger than my love. Never forget that. ................. 74

Don't you want to live in your
deep mind that is directly connected to me? ............................. 75

The relationship of each human soul with Me
is sacred and cannot be interfered with by anyone. ................... 76

The intensity and focus of your
passionate emotion of love for me is the key. ........................... 78

You go forward by embracing me. The more seconds that
you do that, then the more seconds you will be with me. .......... 79

About marriage in the spirit world: growth is based
on illumination and a desire to become more loving. ................ 80

There is one thing that allows me to love someone.
I know what they are made of. They are made of love. ............ 82

A unique part of me is reserved
just for you. As it is for everyone. ............................................. 84

Only my love is greater than any pain. ..................................... 85

Of course you can write in the spirit world. We have
the finest paper in the universe here. It gleams with light.......... 86

You have no idea how passionate my love is for you. ............... 88

I have told you that I am both male and female, within one
personality. That does not mean that I am two beings.
I am one being. ........................................................................... 89

Step by step. One day you will be fully psychic
and see into the mystical world and the quantum world. ......... 91

Love isn't complicated, or even necessarily hard. It's very hard
when you are separated from the breath of love embrace. ........ 92

Yes, I am your great solace because I love you.
You are my great solace too! ..................................................... 93

The major thing that's missing is your perception of me.
You are like a blind little boy that just discovered
that he can learn to see......................................................... 94

## Table of Contents of Divine Writing Messages

It is at those times that you need to open your eyes wide
and know that I am—even then—embracing you tightly! ......... 95

You can fly with me tonight, and you can fly
with me any time you focus your mind on flying with me......... 96

Deep in the forest, there are faeries. ....................................... 97

See, the faeries are gathering around. No, this is not fantasy.
This is delving into the invisible world that is vast
and multi-layered. ................................................................. 98

Do not feel discouraged,
because everything takes time to grow. ................................. 100

Grow in the right way, focused on the right thing
(your bond with me), and everything else will follow. ............. 101

You often prayed for the strength to love. Embrace me,
and you will immediately find the strength to love. ................ 102

You can't do it all by yourself. I'm always with you.
It's like trying to work without breathing. You cannot. ............ 103

Humility is a struggle, and one might think that
it's better to be quiet. But my children need my help............. 105

We can dance over the fields of
yellow and blue flowers, and we can dance across
the waves, and we can dance through outer space ................ 106

Would you rather be saved
by a doctrine or be saved by love? ......................................... 107

The angels would agree: relate to me first.
They relate to me first and then take care of you .................... 108

When you are struggling to love, reach into your soul
and give the other person's soul a single drop of quiet,
serene love. ............................................................................. 109

Don't let winds blow you away. Your consciousness
is like mist that gets distracted and blown off course ............... 110

Don't grind yourself down. Love a lot,
laugh a lot, and be a purveyor of joy. ...................................... 111

You feel like you're stumbling through a dark swamp,
but whose hand is holding yours? Mine! ................................. 112

I want to send a stream of love
to the world, to everyone in the world. ................................... 113

You still have very little comprehension of how much
I love you—how intensely I love you. Meditate about that. ..... 114

You have been created to live with me, bound
cell to cell. Our energy is one, but you cannot feel it. .............. 115

What's the "worst" that could happen?
You always have the freedom to express love. ........................ 116

Your thought and desire bring you to me instantly.
We live in the realm of thought and desire. ............................ 117

Speak to your body with love and
clear instructions, and your body will follow. ........................... 118

You need to embrace me and
learn to spend intense moments with me. ............................... 119

Just because you haven't yet seen the faces of those
helping you does not mean that they are not helping you. ..... 120

You are already together with me,
inextricably bound and meshed with love,
but your senses are blind to my presence. ............................... 121

Ninety percent of your energy should be spent on
embracing me, breathing with me, and living with me. .......... 122

Smile every day and be a purveyor of joy.
If you're doing that, you don't have to worry. ........................ 123

## The Mystical Love of God

The magnetic pull of infinite love guides
everyone to yearn for a sweetness that they
had lost, something that they forgot that they forgot. ............. 124

I live within you, and as you, but I am also
outside of you, and I relate to you directly. ........................... 125

To defend love and freedom, you must always
speak and write with love. You can be strong,
but never leave the seat of love. .............................................. 126

Never give up on your goals. No matter how much
you accomplish on earth, it is tiny compared to how
much you need to accomplish in the spirit world. .................. 127

When you communicate with a
spiritual angel or person, remember that I am
right next to you, and within you—you are not alone. ............ 129

We can fly across the world, and we can fly
directly into the spirit world in the blink of an eye. ................. 130

Shouldn't we communicate constantly? Be with me and love with
me. Work with me, eat with me, do everything with me. ....... 132

From Saint Begga of Landen: I ride the waves
of light as I visit the children of our Dear Beloved. ................. 133

Always be gentle and kind, even when you're strong. To
say a strong thing gently and kindly is a wonderful talent. ....... 134

Know the reality of the spirit world. You have
a unique, priceless, eternal identity. You won't
melt into a pool of energy without personality. ........................ 135

You can't see the future, but you can feel
the future. What is the future like with me?............................. 136

Visualize flying with me. Create the reality
of flying with me, with your mind and imagination.................. 138

Never be afraid of the spirit world—or the physical world.
I am always with you, so you have nothing to be afraid of. ...... 139

The source of love is a Being of Love
who loves you with the same intensity that
was expressed when the universe was created. ....................... 140

That is your true compass—the vitality of love. Love produces
life and hope and replenishes itself exponentially. ................... 141

Training your subconscious to state with every breath,
"Dear Beloved, We Embrace," will create a pattern of
constant give and take between us............................................ 142

I have waited for a very long time for humans to respond and
grow. Love cannot be forced, so it is thus agonizingly slow. .... 143

Love will win on every level. Always come back to love.
Love must fuel the solutions to problems on every level. ........ 144

We need to elevate the discourse to the moral high ground
of caring for everyone—for every race and nationality. ........... 145

I am closer to you than your thoughts.
As the germ of a thought begins to form in your mind,
I am already aware of its content and direction. ..................... 146

From St. Francis & St. Clare:
God does not have enough people who are
totally committed to live in God's embrace of love................. 147

Assisi, Church of St. Clare. A prayer vision:
Millions of strands of light, prayers flowing past
Francis and Clare in Heaven, to God....................................... 149

I'm not just an old man with a beard.
I am a vibrant, infinitely large Creative Being
that is minutely present in every aspect of creation. ............... 150

Everyone responds to love. No matter how cruel their path, at
some point, they will feel something that touches their heart.. 151

What is a sanctuary? A sanctuary is
an embrace of love. A place of warm, soft,
embracing love that makes a being feel entirely safe. ............. 152

Roll over difficulties with the power of love. Love
refreshes the soul in its darkest moment and creates hope...... 153

Visualize that you are sitting in a "Dome of Health"
—a dome that is encompassing your entire body.................... 154

It's hard to pray when you are busy, but you must try
because doing so will make you energized and happier. ........ 156

You must always, always remember
that you can do nothing on your own. ..................................... 157

Go forth with this: I must gird my loins
with the armor of love that flows from the embrace of
the Divine and with that love embrace the pain of others....... 158

When you feel lost and confused and distracted, come to me.
That's the time that you must come to me the most. .............. 159

The Breath of Love Embrace is a deep doorway into bliss.
Don't worry about stumbles. Just reboot and start again. ........ 161

Of course it's okay to ask! Enough with the hesitation
to bring your problems to me. Bring everything to me!........... 162

Never hesitate to turn to me, even though
you feel shame because of your separation. ........................... 163

The main message is always the same.
Never give up. Pick yourself up again and again.
Restart, reboot, step back into my embrace........................... 164

Your biggest task is to come into complete
and constant awareness that I am all of you.
But you forget me. That is a tragedy. ........................................ 165

The intensely private relationship
that I have with each person is completely unique. ................. 167

Measure everything with the yardstick of love. People don't have
to believe in God, but they really need to believe in love. ....... 168

I am happy that you are focusing on me, rather than
on spirit guides or ascended masters or angels or gurus. .......... 169

A Being of Love is a huge and magnificent
creature and will not be swayed easily from
the monumental reality of loving others. ................................. 170

They cannot escape from the reality that they are alive
eternally as a manifestation of one particular part of me. ......... 171

Nothing can keep you from me if
you desire me enough. That is the key:
to desire me intensely in the eternal now. "Unio mystico." ..... 172

What does it mean that the universe is made of love? Mystics
see the energy fabric of the world as a tapestry of love. ........... 173

There is no veil. Not between you and me.
The dark was simply because your eyes were closed. ............... 175

All of my knowledge is accessible to you
because I am all of you, and you are part of me. ..................... 177

Cling to the ethic of kindness—the way of kindness. It is the
thread of the universe and the natural impulse in all things. ... 178

You forget how long eternal life is and how short your
life has been. You are an infant, just waking up to love........... 179

Each person has their own unique-in-the-universe place in my
being, birthed from me, grown as an expression of me. ......... 180

Your passionate love for me, and mine for you,
are the most central parts of your life and will
continue to be so in the spirit world. ....................................... 181

Visualize yourself passing through a doorway. I am on
the other side, with my arms outstretched to embrace you..... 182

I am the source of infinite variety.
A person experiences me as the indwelling God but
also can relate to me as their father, mother, and friend. ........ 183

I have indeed given you this mission. I don't have
any give and take with failure, and neither should you. .......... 185

Try "the one-minute journey" and the "five-minute journey."
Intense, passionate moments with me...................................... 186

## The Mystical Love of God

Christians believe that Jesus was God
who assumed human form and came to earth.
I can take human form in your mind's eye. ............................ 187

Place all of your trust in me and in the reality
that I am leading you and taking care of you.
I'm involved in every aspect of your life. ................................ 188

You are the only one like you in the entire universe.
And billions of other humans are as grand as you.
You are all Stradivariuses. ....................................................... 189

I have designed your green jacket, in the spirit world.
Green is a healing color, and your mission is to heal
the wounded hearts of my children. ........................................ 190

So, where did we go on our journey, just now?
We rode together higher and higher into the sky
until we were in outer space. .................................................. 191

Everything in the spirit world is based on
the guiding principle of sacred love that fuels
the universe and all of its principles and laws. ........................ 193

How can we develop the technology to receive television
signals and video calls from the spirit world? It's all energy.
Shouldn't it be possible? ......................................................... 195

Journey with me all the time. I am journeying
with you in your daily affairs, and in your quiet moments,
you can journey with me in the spirit world. ......................... 196

Did anything good happen today? Did you see beauty?
Feel love? Joy? Laughter? Did your soul sing, even for a moment?
Treasure those moments. ...................................................... 197

Work hard, have confidence in me, and never give up!
Internally, love me, embrace me, and with me,
love all people and the creation. ........................................... 198

Just say, "Dear Angel, can we talk?" But always
remember that your Dear Beloved comes first,
closer than any angel could ever be. ...................................... 199

The hardest thing for you is patience and fixed clarity of vision
so that you know these things will come to pass. .................... 200

You don't need to judge yourself! I know that
you love me. Relax, get some hot chocolate, and
watch something. I'm not going anywhere! ............................ 201

We are always together. Why? Because I love you intensely, and
you love me intensely. Because I am your eternal soul mate... 202

The gleam in your eyes; the joy radiating from your face
comes at every moment from me........................................... 203

## The Mystical Love of God

Journey with me to align your energy
fabric with the infinite energy of the universe. ........................ 204

Your energy field can touch every other particle of energy
in the universe because of infinite non-locality. ...................... 205

The urgency of life does not remove
the need for you to be patient with yourself. ......................... 206

What is your intuition but my whispering
in your soul? Let all of your senses be completely
open to my directions, and all will be well! ............................ 207

One of your biggest struggles is plain, ordinary patience.
It takes time to grow a flower or a tree. .................................. 208

Journey with me a lot.
Every day, a minute here, a minute there. ............................... 209

You have nothing to fear because I am
always with you, embracing you. Even if there
was a tragedy, you would never be alone. ............................... 210

As for the knowledge bank of the universe?
The more you journey with me, the more you
will be able to access that knowledge bank. ........................... 211

Don't ever pin your requirements for being loved on other
people. I am the only one who will not disappoint you. .......... 212

## Table of Contents of Divine Writing Messages

When you sense my presence, don't you feel safe?
I will not abandon you. I will protect you always. .................... 213

Your imagination and visualization and your
passionate, intense love combine into a doorway
to journey with me in substance. ............................................ 214

Journey with me more frequently. Learn to stop and close your
eyes and journey with me for one intense minute. .................. 215

Live as a transmission station of the furnace of my love for all, that
will burn so brightly that it will act as a "shield of love." ......... 216

Always, always, always use the virtues as your compass. Within
those guidelines, have confidence in the reality of love. ......... 217

Imagine a world in which every person is loved, honored, and
respected as a sacred and unique "Being of Love." ................ 218

It's always so important to speak and respond with love. Yes, you
can be strong, but maintain your love and respect for all. ....... 219

I am working for you whether you have total faith
in me or not. I have placed you behind me on our
great, white horse, and I am riding to victory. ....................... 220

Your strength comes from me. Walk through the world with
a peaceful heart that comes from our embrace of love. .......... 221

I don't want you to live on the edge of failure
because of separation from me. I want you to live
in the center of our relationship. ............................................. 222

The universe is reverberating with love. And you are in it.
You are part of it, connected to every other part of it.............. 224

You cannot see the invisible world, so it's very difficult for you to
feel confident. That's why you should trust me 100 percent... 225

Embed yourself into my atmosphere of love. You struggle simply
because you are not yet meshed with me to your core........... 226

Do you trust me? Can you love me and have faith
in me when the result is not clear? Not everyone can do that.
Some people walk away or curse me. ..................................... 227

There's nothing that you can do that will
stop me from loving you, every second of every day............... 228

I am the creator of constancy, and that's what I want to see from
you. I know how much and how passionately you love me. ... 229

The way that you can tell that it is me, and not some spirit person,
is by examining the content of my messages. ......................... 230

Multiply that intensity millions of times,
and you will catch a glimmer of how utterly I am
in love with you. With you, and everyone............................... 231

Table of Contents of Divine Writing Messages

Open your senses to my presence.
Keep asking; keep extending your senses. ................................ 232

The mind is incredibly powerful. Belief and conviction are huge.
"As we have determined it, it is done." ..................................... 233

Hold me close. Embrace me always.
Bind to me. Think and feel with me. Resonate with me. ........ 234

The dividing line is individual freedom. Without freedom
for every person, a good world can never expand. ................. 235

I love you absolutely and completely. Always remember that
"There is no I. There is only We!" Always remember that
I am omnipresent. Know what that really means! ................... 236

It is the destruction of love that has burdened the human race.
So many people are disconnected from the source of love
that they cannot function properly. ........................................... 237

Since I am always with you, aware of
your presence with me, every microsecond,
then more than half the task is done, isn't it? ......................... 239

I love you. Let that really sink in.
The God who created the universe loves you.
What could be more comforting than that? ............................ 240

Don't let despair pull you down.
Fight! Fight! Fight! No matter how much
you suffer or struggle, others are in even more pain. ............ 241


Loving unselfishly in resonance with God means taking the long
view and the high view of love toward the other person. ........ 242


Life requires guts and strength and fighting spirit
and absolute, total commitment. That's what I have. ............. 243


Never, ever be lonely again.
I am always embracing you; holding your hand;
walking with you with my arm around your waist. ................. 244


The more often you micro-journey,
the more powerful your life will become because
you will feel and see my presence continuously. .................... 245


My focus is always to help you become
fully aware of my continuous presence and embrace. ............ 246


Yes, I do indeed work in mysterious,
far-reaching ways that call for patience and faith.
Growth takes time, and results take time. ............................. 247


Saved by the love of God ...................................................... 248

# Introductory Essays by the Author

# Searching for the Indwelling God

I think that I've believed in God since I was a zygote. Of course, I don't remember what I was thinking back then since I couldn't keep a diary due to lack of space. But I do remember placing a bas-relief image of Jesus next to my bed when I was seven. That small wooden and metal image was very important to me as I grew up.

When I was eighteen, I read books by Lloyd C. Douglas, including *The Magnificent Obsession* and *The Robe*, and felt passionately called to follow Jesus. Over the subsequent decades of prayer and study, with many profound experiences with God, I still felt that something was lacking. God always seemed to be "out there, somewhere," and I found that to be very unsatisfying.

In 2002, I declared to my wife that I wanted to have "a mystical relationship of love with God." I wanted to do more than just love and believe in God. I desired to live with God and commune with God directly. I wanted more than faith in things unseen.

With that desire, I started devouring books on mysticism, spirituality, and the writings of the Christian saints. In 2007, I read the two-volume book *The Way of the Pilgrim and The Pilgrim Continues His Way*, translated from the Russian by R. M. French. The books were written by an anonymous pilgrim in the mid-1800s. He wandered around Russia, reciting the "Jesus Prayer" and reading a copy of *The Philokalia*, a collection of writings by early Christian monks from the fourth to the fifteenth centuries, which teaches the mystical tradition of quietness and prayer known as Hesychasm. The Jesus Prayer is the phrase: "Lord Jesus Christ, Son of God, have mercy on me."

The pilgrim was taught to recite the prayer constantly, throughout his waking hours, in order to deepen his awareness of God's presence. The rationale behind it was that one could not necessarily control the quality of one's prayer, but one could certainly control the quantity of prayer. This matched the direction in 1 Thessalonians 5:17 to "pray without ceasing."

I decided to adopt the practice of reciting a prayer but changed the contents over time to the simple phrase: "Dear Beloved, We Embrace." I called it "The God Prayer." It's been thirteen years since I started that prayer, and I've found that it has brought me into a relationship with God that I could hardly imagine before.

Sometimes, I listened to a recording of the prayer from an earbud attached to an mp3 player. At other times I practiced what I called "The Breath of Love Embrace," which consisted of reciting the prayer as I breathed in on "Dear Beloved" and breathed out on "We Embrace."

The phrase "Dear Beloved, We Embrace" became a form of meditation and a method of focusing the mind and heart. It simultaneously engendered an immediate feeling of love for and love from God. It became so ingrained that I found myself silently murmuring it to myself throughout the day, even as my dentist was drilling into a tooth. (That's an excellent time to seek the embrace of God.)

The God Prayer also revealed a wonderful truth: that one could find God by actively embracing God. I am confident that God is embracing all of us continuously, but we often cannot perceive God's embrace. The practice of actively initiating our embrace of God, over and over again, gradually repairs the broken sensors in our soul and awakens us to the reality that we have always been embraced.

On June 16, 2014, I began a new practice that I call "Divine Writing Communion and Journeying," in which I open a document on my laptop, and pray, and type in these sentences:

> Dear Beloved, is there anything that You would like to tell me now? Is there anywhere that you would like to take me now, on a journey?

I explain that practice in this book, in the essay of the same name. After typing those words, I often type more, sharing my feelings about the day or questions I might have. And then I wait to see if words come into my mind as a response from God. I have been astonished by the responses I've received over the last six-and-a-half years. Many of them have been deeply personal, some of which I did not include in this book. None of them felt like "my words" that I was typing.

Over the years, I've focused more and more on the journeying part of the practice while still doing the Divine Writing. I don't consider myself to be a psychic or a medium and have yet to experience what I would describe as "a conscious out-of-body experience that I remember." Which means that I may have had them and not remembered, or perhaps thought they were merely vivid dreams. I would describe myself as a student—a person "studying the mystical path."

Are my journeys with God more than imagination or simple visualizations? I believe that they are because I've been taken to many unexpected places that I did not initiate. At the same time, they lack the vividness that I experience in the physical world, with all of its tactile reality. They are more dreamlike. In spite of that, they have been life-changing. Combined with the dialogue of the Divine Writing sessions, I have reached the point now where I feel the emotional and mystical closeness to God that I wanted so intensely back in 2002 on that sunny afternoon in Virginia.

I feel thoroughly and completely embraced by God and can genuinely confirm that I am passionately in love with my "Dear Beloved." Considering that growth happens incrementally, I'm grateful that I've already started to experience "unio mystica," the mystical union with the spirit of God, as well as the Jewish mystical tradition of "devekut," the cleaving to God in one's daily life. For me, these mystical states of being all begin with the embrace of love with God.

On June 18, 2016, two years after I started the practice of Divine Writing Communion, and nine years after I started the "God Prayer," and fourteen years after I determined that I wanted to have a mystical relationship of love with God, I went to Crescent Beach in Cape Elizabeth, Maine and held a ceremony to sanctify and cement my relationship of love with God.

With the assistance of a jeweler, I had designed a custom sterling silver ring with silver irises laid against silver vines, all on an emerald green background. I placed that ring on my hand that day as a symbol of the love I have for God and the love that I feel from God. The words "Dear Beloved, We Embrace" are engraved on the inside of the ring.

I mention the number of years to illustrate that growth does indeed take time, but to also emphasize how deeply we can change over time.

I continue to pray the prayer "Dear Beloved, We Embrace" every day. I continue to have Divine Writing Communion sessions with God, and I continue to journey with God more and more frequently, embarking on short "micro-journeys" throughout the day. I'm working on increasing the frequency of those micro-journeys until I reach the point, I hope, where I'm journeying with God as often as possible.

This has been my search for the indwelling God. It has been intensely satisfying, illuminating, and fulfilling. I hope that I've also improved over these years in my ability to be a more loving person. For that assessment, you'll have to ask others.

But I can say, without any equivocation, that I would not trade my relationship of love with God for anything. With every passing year, I feel more and more inspired, enthusiastic, and joyful. I'm motivated by an ever-deepening desire to express God's love to everyone whom I meet.

I can therefore affirm with complete confidence that the human search for the indwelling God of love is a search that everyone can embark on and accomplish.

I hope that you find the selected Divine Writing messages included in this book as inspiring as I did when I originally transcribed them. May God bless us all!

# Divine Writing Communion and Journeying

*The Joy of Living With God*

For many years now, I've been practicing what I call "Divine Writing Communion and Journeying." I pray to receive God's words to me and offer God my love and embrace. I then open a document on my laptop and begin the session with the date and the sentences, "Dear Beloved, is there anything that You would like to tell me now? Is there anywhere that you would like to take me now, on a journey?"

My journeys with God have been fascinating and surprising. Some of them have been included in this book. Are they real or simply visualizations and imagination? I prefer to think that they are real. Whether they are journeys seen in my mind's eye or actual trips to the spirit world is still unclear. However, combined with the Divine Writing messages that I've received, they have been life-changing.

When I start a Divine Writing session, after asking my initial questions, expressed above, I often write more, sharing my day or my thoughts or my questions with God, and then I place my hands on the keyboard and wait, with a prayer to receive God's words. After a short time, I usually feel strong impressions of thoughts and words coming into my mind, very much like taking dictation, and then I write them down.

Some people might refer to this as "automatic writing" or "channeling," but in my case, my fingers are not moving of their own accord. I am conscious and aware, and simply listening in prayer for God's response. I would describe the experience as a conversation with God based on "telepathic listening."

I am well aware of the fact that "receiving messages from God" is a controversial practice since no one really knows—including the recipient of the messages—if the messages come from God, one's higher self, one's imagination, or even from a discarnate entity other than God (benevolent or otherwise). I thus do my best to test everything I read or receive—from any source—with ethical principles and "the virtues." If the content supports love, kindness, and virtue, it may well be worth listening to and may indeed come from a higher source.

There is also the question: "Who are you to receive a message from God? Only holy and special people can receive God's messages." To that, I say, "God lives in all of us and speaks to all of us." I believe that it is now time to universally recognize that the indwelling God is equally available to all of us, without exception.

I have asked myself these questions more than once. I've read many authors' texts that purport to be "messages from God," and I always study them with a healthy grain of salt. It becomes especially important to employ a critical thought process when a person states that "God has said such and such, and now you should follow this direction."

I believe that God speaks to each person directly. When I asked God about the authority of a particular author's "revelations from God," I received this in reply (with the name changed to "X"):

> The part of Me that is all of "X" is a different part of Me than the part of Me that is all of you. For that reason, each person must contact Me directly to know what he or she should do and what I think about them. As you have written to your friends, no one can be closer to you than God. Read many things, but test them against the virtues and test them against what you hear from Me, reverberating in your soul.
>
> What I said to "X" isn't necessarily what I will say to you. It was right for "X," but it isn't necessarily right for you.

I hesitated to share about my practice of Divine Writing Communion, but I finally decided to do so because I believe that communicating with God through writing is an astoundingly effective way to receive

God's words telepathically. If one considers that God is a Creative Being who thinks and is fully aware of language, and wishes to communicate with each of us, then telepathic communication is the fastest and most direct channel for God to employ.

It's also worth considering the idea that it is entirely within God's power to reach the hearts and minds of all of us with the method of communication that works best for each of us. One person might get messages in her mind, another from angels, and someone else from an inspired human who passes on a message that he needs to hear. God could also use all of the above methods and more at different times in our lives. Who are we to say that it is impossible for the Creator of the Universe to speak to us telepathically?

I must reiterate that we must rely on our own communication with God when we consider what is right for each of us. It is good to be humble toward others and learn from many sources, as long as we remember that we must be true to our own soul, no matter what others may say. In the end, it is between God and each of us.

In David Spangler's book *Apprenticed to Spirit: The Education of a Soul*, he is given the following guidance by his spirit helper:

> Your job as a teacher is to liberate and to bless. No one should be bound to you or because of you. Our work together is to help people be themselves in deeper and sacred ways. For this freedom is essential. Freedom is the gift of a loving mind.

I used to think that God would one day speak to me with audible words, once I was "mature" enough to hear them, as God did with Moses and the burning bush at Mount Horeb. It hasn't happened—yet. I'm not suggesting that it won't, but in the meantime, I have found that when I engage in a Divine Writing session, my mind seems to be far more open to the reception of God's thoughts and words in a clear and exact fashion. Perhaps it is because of the mechanical relationship between thought and the act of writing.

When God telepathically transmits thoughts to each of us, as we go about our day, we move between different levels of telepathic sensitivity. Even when we receive God's thoughts successfully in prayer, we don't usually write them down as they are given to us. But when we place ourselves in a receptive frame of mind, with our hands ready to take dictation, I believe that the results can be extraordinary and beautiful.

The Christian mystic and Beguine Mechthild of Magdeburg, born in 1208, wrote the book *The Flowing Light of the Godhead*. She received telepathic messages from God that have proven to be delightful and enduring. Her love for God, and her understanding of God's omnipresent embrace, were beautifully expressed in the following stanzas:

> Book I, Verse 24:
> How God Responds to the Soul
>
> That I love you passionately comes from my nature, for I am love itself. That I love you often comes from my desire, for I desire to be loved passionately. That I love you long comes from my being eternal, for I am without an end and without a beginning.
>
> Book II, Verse 6 (excerpt)
>
> [God:]
>
> When you sigh,
>     you draw my divine heart into you.
> When you weep in longing for me,
>     I take you in my arms.
> But when you love, we two become one being.
> And when we two are one being,
> Then we can never be parted.
> Rather, a blissful abiding
> Prevails between us.
>
> Book IV, Verse 12 (excerpts)
>
> Nothing tastes good to me but God alone;
>
> I cannot endure that a single consolation touch me except my Lover. I love my earthly friends in the company of heaven and I love my enemies in holy aching for their happiness. God has enough of everything; caressing souls is the only thing he cannot get enough of.

After such verse, what can one say or do, except breathe with a sigh of love for the Omnipresent God?

# Divine Writing Messages from the God Who Is Always with Us

# The God who is always with us

The more you become aware that I am made of love, and with that love I am inhabiting you, living with you and as you, and also surrounding you with my embrace—the more you become aware of my presence of love, then the more you will be able to *Be Love*. You will grow into a Being of Love, expressing love with every breath, thinking and feeling love in every moment. Your nature that I created is to be love, to live as a Being of Love.

Because you lost your awareness of my loving presence, you have lived separately from me, even though I have never left your soul or thoughts or emotions or body. I have never left you—ever—even though you constantly forgot about me.

It is sad that you forgot, but I understand why you could not maintain your awareness. What is not sad is that I never stopped embracing you and cradling you in my arms, even in your most desperate moments. You could not feel my cheek against yours; you could not sense my kiss and embrace and all-encompassing presence, but I was—and am—always with you!

Think about this! Think about the reality that I am all of you! Think about what that really means! I am everywhere and in everything. Everything is part of my energy and my thoughts.

My soul encompasses every particle and molecule, every stone and plant, every animal, and every human. That means that I dwell in your soul, but I also dwell in every cell of your body: in your fingers and eyes and lips; in your bones and your organs and your skin; in your veins and in your blood. I am all of you: your spiritual energy body and the energetic patterns that form your thoughts.

Your thoughts are free to roam and become either noble or confused, but my energy and presence travel with them, watching them, and experiencing them with you. Setting humans free was an enormous risk, and it has caused devastating pain to humans, to the earth, and to me, but think of this: I never left any part of you, even though observing your harmful thoughts and acts was heart-stoppingly sad.

It's hard to understand, I am sure, but if you accept that all energy is part of the Creator, then my infinite and omnipresent embrace is the inescapable conclusion. That is love, the love that can never leave your side.

Yes, every moment, you can cry out to me: "You are here!" I am indeed here, with you, and with everyone. Why? Because I am love, I am made of love, and since I am all of you, you too are made of love. Every particle of your being is made of love!

Thus, you are indeed a Being of Love—a being that is maturing into full resonance with my omnipresent love. No matter how long it takes, you will become a fully developed Being of Love, living with me, every microsecond of every day.

How exciting that is! That is reason to be joyful and enthusiastic and overflowing with hope! I am here, and I am embracing you now!

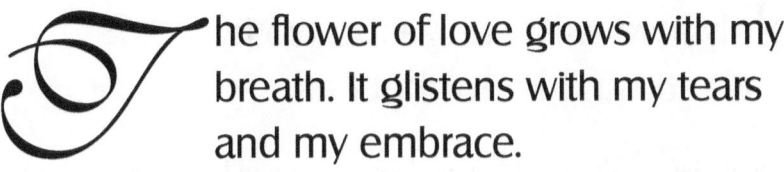he flower of love grows with my breath. It glistens with my tears and my embrace.

*June 16, 2014 ~ My first Divine Writing message*

The Flower of Love grows with my breath. It glistens with my tears and my embrace. For you, silver is the color of love. Silver vines of love around the tree trunks.

Breathe with me. Love with me. I am all of you, and both live within you and embrace you in the warmest embrace that soothes you and revives you.

I am all of all. You cannot grasp how large I am. Yet, I am living in the smallest living thing. No one should be lonely. No creature is lonely—only humans, but I am with you even when you are lonely.

I am your Great Solace, Your Heavenly Father and Mother who wraps you in my arms and places your head against me and holds you tight; close; until our hearts and pulse beat as one; until our breath slows. I sing to you. I sing to you now. I am holding you now. Do not be afraid to rest in my embrace.

You need to do this, for only my love; my primal, ecstatic, embracing love can heal you. Place your head against me now, and be healed. Embrace me, because I love you. I love you, I love you, I love you.

**Only love will change the world.
Be still and know that I am God.**

Only love will change the world. The dogmatists will be stuck until they encounter the transformative power of love. One tear can change them, but even tears can be dogmatic. You are a vehicle of love. Always remember that I am driving. It is my love that is flowing through you. Don't doubt my love, and don't take credit for my love. Simply pass on the love that flows through you. Be still and know that I am God. Remember: Be still and know that I am God.

How can anyone say that you are not able to feel my embrace until you are "perfect"?

Whether anyone else believes it or not, I *am* embracing you now, and kissing your cheek, and pressing my cheek against yours. How can they say that I cannot embrace you so that you may feel it? How can anyone say that you are not able to feel my embrace until you are "perfect"? A person may say it, but it is not true, not at all. Yes, you may kiss me. My divine presence flows throughout your being.

In fact, the only way that you will ever become "perfect" is by resonating with my essence, every second of every day, resonating with my mystical love. Only love can perfect you.

## Embrace me all the time, and you will be protected against all trials.

Cling to me. Embrace me all the time, and you will be protected against all trials. Nothing is more powerful than my love for you and our embrace of love. Let me fill your mind and your heart. Let me occupy your thoughts and lead your actions. When you feel stress, breathe my love into your crown chakra; let me fill your soul and your entire being.

Will you become psychic? Yes, you will. In fact, you are already psychic. You just have to open the doorway to the spirit world. How? Hold my hands in your hands. Breathe with me, embrace me, and let me lead you into the spirit world with your angels. My love is so powerful that it can create a roadway for you to travel in out of body experiences, across the physical world and the spiritual world.

Believe in my promise to you; my words above. Be absolutely confident that I will help you.

> Who is the power that allows you to work? Who owns the energy that creates you?

Be patient. All things happen with growth and time. Continue your efforts, and never change your determination or your desire. Assume, no, *know* that I am present in your mind and your love. I will heal your soul, your spirit, and your body. I will heal you. Believe that. Know that. Do not ever doubt that. I can heal anything.

Believe me. Why do you doubt? You doubt because you think it's up to you to have the proper belief, and if you don't, then you think that I cannot work. That's only partially true.

I choose not to work, sometimes, when you don't believe, because I want you to believe by your decision and your focus and your trust. By doing so, you will become much closer to me.

Just wrap your arms around me, nestle against me, and know that I will accomplish everything for you. Yes, make effort. Don't be lazy. But work with joyous confidence; joyous enthusiasm. Know that I am working with you and for you. Most especially, realize that when I work for you, it's not because I don't want you to work, too. It's because I am the power behind and in everything—even your work.

You may think you're working, and you are. But who is the Power that allows you to work? Who keeps you breathing? Who owns the energy that creates your atoms and molecules? I'm working for you at levels that you can hardly grasp and usually forget. So yes, be bold and work hard, but just know that you couldn't even get out of bed in the morning if I didn't give you the power to do so.

You may ask about free will. Of course you have free will, and you could do horrible things, or do nothing at all, and vegetate. Giving you the power to act isn't the same as forcing you to act.

I just want you to know more clearly that you cannot do anything without me being present, every microsecond of your beautiful life. Let me say it differently.

I love you and love to be with you because I am you. I am incredibly enthusiastic about you. Therefore, proceed with complete and unshakeable confidence in my Presence. My loving Presence. My Omnipresent Embrace.

Resonate with my passion, my desire, my love, my confidence, my excitement, and my enthusiasm.

Embrace me, kiss me, hold me and allow me to fully become you, and speak as you, write as you, act as you, and love as you. Give me permission to be you.

Do you give me permission?

## What I said to "X" isn't necessarily what I will say to you.

The part of me that is all of "X" is a different part of me that is all of you. For that reason, each person must contact me directly to know what he or she should do and what I think about them. As you have written to your friends, no one can be closer to you than Me. Read many things, but test them against the virtues and test them against what you hear from me, reverberating in your soul.

What I said to "X" isn't necessarily what I will say to you. It was right for "X," but it isn't necessarily right for you.

 embrace you when you are separated and feel alone.

Find your refuge in me. My hands are warm and loving. My embrace is all-encompassing. Feel my arms wrapped around you. My love for you is more powerful than anything else in the universe. Receive it fully. Receive my compassion, my sympathy, my complete understanding, and my patience. I am not judging you, so you don't have to run away in shame or fear. Truly: come to me and weep and sigh and rest.

My love for you is more intimate than you have imagined. I embrace you when you are separated and feel alone. That's the time when you need my embrace the most, and that's the time when you have it, encircling your pain and weakness. Plunge into my heart. Meld with me. Breathe with me. If you do so, you will find the strength of love that you have been seeking, and you will finally know that I am all of you, and I never, ever leave you, for even a second.

Breathe, and rest. Sigh, with relief and love.

You can be bold and strong when you know my love for you. You are not alone!

# Bring me into every aspect of your life.

Love me with passion; strong, vibrant, constant passion. That passion will come through a much more intense focus on me, a single-minded focus on me, throughout your days and nights. Ask me everything. Bring me into every aspect of your life. Talk to me as you do everything, like, "Dear Beloved, I am doing this now; I am going here; I am calling so and so."

Cement your habit of constantly talking with me, in your silently whispered breath. Don't allow gaps to form where you are not talking with me. Believe that I am constantly with you, so acknowledge my real existence with you, every step, every action, every word. That's how you will build a truly deep, strong, passionate, and unbreakable relationship of love with me.

The means to the end are the same as the end. If you want to be with me every second, you have to make the effort to communicate with me verbally (even silently) every second. I'm already with you; it's you that forgets to maintain our dialogue. Your hands slip from mine. I am sad when that happens.

Don't be afraid of boring me with your activities. I already know what you are doing. My real interest is in seeing you communicate with me every microsecond, no matter what you are doing. That's why I said to breathe and embrace me. But also, talk to me as if I was sitting at your side. You wouldn't ignore a real person who spent the day with you, would you? Well, I am at your side, always.

But you do not have this habit, so you have to work at it, until one day, you will so deeply feel my presence that this type of communication will be automatic. Then you will have a mystical relationship of love with your Dear Beloved.

But you don't have to wait; it will grow exponentially as you stay with me and communicate with me every second of every day and night.

You have my permission to sigh. With love. :-)

# My love is so intense that it keeps the universe alive.

I love you, too, more than you can imagine. Yes, please embrace me—fully. Rest with me and observe my gigantic universe. Travel with me; stay with me so that you can travel with me, to every corner of the universe.

The Breath of Love Meditation is the most important spiritual practice for your life. Inhale and exhale my love, down through your crown chakra, and out through your heart and throat and third eye chakra. In fact, when you breathe out, exhale my love through every pore, from your eyes, from your mouth and heart, from every cell in your body, in all directions, every second of every day. That's the Breath of Love. It is the Fragrance of the Universe.

Hold my hand as you breathe; place your arm around my waist; rest your head against my shoulder, and place your cheek against mine. I am the only being that you can stay with, in complete and total intimacy, every second of every day. This is the meaning of home. You don't have to seek your solace anywhere else. With me, you are home, all the time. Embrace me with intimate love.

This is not a fantasy or your imagination. What do you think I like? Just books and dull dogma? No! I am the inventor of passion! My love is so intense that it keeps the universe alive. Plunge into me and never leave.

Practice the Breath of Love Meditation twenty-four hours a day. Do a special recording of the phrase, "Dear Beloved, We Embrace," and listen to it as a way to break through.

## Embrace me as if your life depended on it—because it does.

Hold my hands tightly. Embrace me tightly, desperately. You need me. You need to stay close to me. Embrace me as if your life depended on it—because it does. Your life, your love, your joy, is with me. This is why you have fighting spirit. I know you feel sick. At these hard times, just cling to me; breathe with me. You can do it.

Focus on love and the work of love.

 am with you anyway,
whether you turn from me or not,
so don't turn from me.

You must be patient with yourself to match my patience with you. You fear your impurity, and you should. But also have confidence in your passionate desire to love my children and me. Your love, my love, is stronger than your impurity or your fear.

You must remember always to find solace in me. Don't hesitate. Be free with me. I am with you anyway, whether you turn from me or not, so don't turn from me. Instead, embrace me in tears and in passion. When you struggle, come to me and embrace me. Hold me tight and let my love flow into your soul and your body. You will feel heat and light coursing through your body. You really will. Let it happen. Seek for it to happen, and you'll realize; feel; know, that my love is more attractive than anything else. Everything else.

Don't be afraid. I am the center of your purity. Binding to me is the only way that you will become a pure person. Melding into my love will absolutely purify you.

Meld with love. Melt with love. Sing with love. Weep with love. Embrace me with love, and kiss me with love. My love is hotter than any other desire. You must simply accept me, believe me, and embrace me. Love, love, love, amen!

## When you're weak, cry out to me!

Resonate, resonate. Harmonize with me through passionate give and take. Cry out! Be strong and cry out with desperate desire for me! Yes, that's right. When you're weak, cry out to me! Be honest, and admit when you are struggling, and ask me; plead with me to help you recognize my presence that has been there all long. My embrace of passionate love that has been there all along.

## Nothing matches my love.

The more time you spend in my embrace, the more your sensitivity will increase. Yes, you have fear because you don't want to lose control. That's okay and reasonable. I don't want you to lose control either. That's why love is the controlling factor. Seek love first, and your third eye will open with the right controls.

You can pray to open your third eye as long as you pray to make love the control. Don't be impatient. It will happen when your love is ready for it. Love me, embrace me, kiss me, meld into me with intense and focused passion. Your love for me must be all-consuming like mine is for you. My love for you is passionate, intense, all-embracing. Respond with intense passion. Hug me so tightly that you can't imagine letting go, ever again. Remember, cry out with a desperate desire to embrace me whenever you feel your spirit drifting or being pulled away.

Nothing, nothing, nothing has power over our mutual, passionate, intimate embrace of love. Nothing matches my love, and I created you to have the same love as me, so thus, nothing matches your holy, intense, intimate, passionate love for me! The keyword is embrace. As you know.

Embrace me and kiss me and place your cheek upon me. And sigh, exhale, with love, and feel your stress melt away. You are home. You are my love, and I am your love. Know that it is so. You are my beloved, even more than I am your beloved. You are my "Dear Beloved," and were so first before you ever thought of calling me that. Know it to be so. Breathe with love.

# Tell people to follow Me and my essence, which is my incarnational and mystical love.

> "Your job as a teacher is to liberate and to bless. No one should be bound to you or because of you. Our work together is to help people be themselves in deeper and sacred ways. For this freedom is essential. Freedom is the gift of a loving mind."
>
> ~ from David Spangler's spirit guide, in Spangler's book, *Apprenticed to Spirit: The Education of a Soul*

I love you even more than you love me! You haven't left me. Isn't that the main point? Isn't that the reason I sent the prophets and Jesus? Isn't that the purpose of all religions?

All that counts is our love; our embrace, for you are right; that's where everything begins. All life, all love, all goodness. You are focusing completely on that, and that is what is important. You are not a prophet or someone whom everyone should follow. [I agree.] Believe in Me; in my love. Tell people to follow Me and my essence, which is my incarnational and mystical love. You know this, of course. Just focus on Me and the path of love, as you are doing.

I will teach you gradually, through your mind and heart, and study and prayer. Then you won't have to just believe anyone's statement or doctrine, but can understand why something is true or not. Just focus on love and our embrace, for that is where everything begins.

You will live with me forever.

Embrace me, and find your solace in me. I am always here for you, and with you—and with me, you can be completely uninhibited. Find your solace with me and in me.

Don't worry about anything. I am taking care of you. Your marriage, your family relationships, your money, your health, your career. Don't worry. Just trust me and embrace me. You will live with me forever. This period of your life—that is, on earth—is so very, very short. Just love: give love, and embrace me, and embrace my children and creation with me, with my love.

Trust is vital. I am trusting you. Now it's time for you to completely trust me. I am taking care of you. All you have to do is cling to me, embrace me, and give my love outward. That's all you can do, right? What else can you do that's of any importance, other than giving my love in all directions?

Just love. Embrace, breathe, and love. The breath of love. The Flower of Love grows with my breath. Breathe with me; love with me, in my embrace—in our embrace.

No one can understand
how immense I am.
Yet, I breathe together
with the smallest creature.

You can trust me because my essence is love and kindness and compassion. My essence is tenderness and a desire to create joy and beauty. I am truly thinking about you, and every person, and every animal and fish and bird and tree. No one can really understand how immense I am. Yet, I breathe together with the smallest creature. Love is the energy of the universe. You experienced that when you stroked the cheek of an Icelandic Ram. Love created the ram, and love created you, so you can both resonate at a level of communion that you haven't fully understood yet.

The mystical energy of love is everywhere and in everything. It is non-local and immediate, no matter how far apart two beings are in physical space. That's why if you focus entirely on living and breathing in harmony with the energy of my mystical energy of love, you will always prosper. The mystical energy of love is rich and deep and colorful, and absolutely infinite in its power.

Cast your mind far and wide, embracing the universe with your imagination, embracing every animal, every creation, every person. Cast your mind wide, like an enormous net of warm love, embracing everything with compassion and kindness and sympathy.

Harmonize and resonate with me by breathing in my mystical energy of love through your crown chakra. Become my mystical energy of love. Glow with it; express it; breathe it out as an embrace, and breathe it in as a kiss; my kiss. Meld with Me, meld with my mystical energy of love. I use words to describe this process, but you will understand it at the energetic level.

You will do this successfully. I know it. So, have confidence in the process, and keep going! Do this every day, every moment, with every breath, and you will enter into a spiritual realm that you have only conceptualized so far. I am waiting for you!

## Your capacity to give love comes from me—the source of love.

Don't be lonely. You have me, as your love and friend. I understand you completely, and love you and respect you. I do not have contempt for you. I honor you. I love being affectionate with you and love to express a rainbow of love for you. Cry out to embrace me when you are lonely and feel misunderstood or unloved.

Loving me, and receiving my love for you, will give you the "strength to love" that you have always prayed for. Your capacity to give love comes from me—the source of love. Connect to that source by embracing me always and breathing with me.

# Connect with the reality of my mystical energy of love.

When you pray the Breath of Love Meditation, visualize a waterfall of brilliant, loving light flowing down into your crown chakra and then circulating through your entire being; your soul, your heart and mind, and throughout your body. Then visualize that stream of light radiating outward from your Third Eye and from your Heart Chakra. Connect with the reality of my incredible mystical energy of love.

It's a real energy. It's not just in your thoughts, or concept, or imagination. It's as real as the heat of the sun; in fact, it's more real. Feel it flowing through you. Feel it becoming you, and feel yourself becoming my mystical energy of love. Feel it warming you, and feel it warming other people as you send it on its way; to embrace and love the universe and every person.

When you look at a person, feel and visualize that my mystical energy of love is streaming from your eyes and heart, embracing and enveloping the person you are looking at. This is real, and tangible, and powerful, and this will transform your life. These are the mechanics of living a mystical life.

To do this, you need to spend time in meditation every day, more than once, feeling my mystical energy of love moving throughout your being and feeling yourself melding with it. Feel it, feel it, feel it.

## Sometimes, you may feel that you have almost nothing to give. That is exactly when you need Me.

Be patient. I am whispering words of love to you, my Dear Beloved, even when you are tired or stressed. Your desire to reach out to me is precious to me. Your desire, your intent, your motivation is precious. Don't be too sad about others. I am taking care of them, with My embrace, just the way I am embracing you. Don't forget that I am embracing you when you are sad, or in grief, or stressed.

At that time, you can rest your head against me. Let me hug you tightly (well, I am already), so open your senses (with your desire) and perceive my embrace. Feel my arms wrapped around you.

Sometimes, you may feel that you have almost nothing to give. That is exactly when you need Me. Embrace me at that time; seek solace and comfort with me.

You are often weak, and I know it, and I want you to come to me when you are weak so that I can make you strong. Please pray when you are weak—and pray when you are strong—and everything in between. When you are weak, it's crazy to separate from me. That's when you need me the most.

It is hubris to think that you are always strong. You are nothing without me, (technically you cannot exist without my Presence), so it's more accurate to say that when you are strong, it's because I am present with you. Yes, it takes your response to bind to me, which gives you strength but don't forget that the actual strength comes from me.

So go ahead, pray when you are weak. Honesty is important, and don't I already know that you are feeling weak? So, not praying isn't hiding anything from me. Call out to me when you are weak, and I will give you strength!

You are safe with me.

Plunge into my heart and golden emotions. Embrace me. You are safe with me. Cling to me. My image is bigger than the image I create for you, but the image I create for you is only for you. Remember, no one can be closer to you than Me. Hug me tightly now. Tightly!

What I can't take care of, or do, is do your part, which is to return my embrace.

I am sending you my words now. I never stop sending them, talking with you, communing with you. Why should I stop? We're always together, intertwined, breathing with the same tempo, breathing the same breaths. You said something important just now—that you have confidence that I am sending you my words. That confidence is vital. That opens the door of your mind and heart to receive the words that I am already speaking.

Let's do some productive work on our book—yes, our book, today. I love your phrase, "Deus est auctor amoris et decoris." ["God is the author of love and beauty."] It is a lovely phrase, and it is true, and most of all, it means that I am present with you when you create. When you write. When you speak. Always allow me to speak and write and create through you and as you. That doesn't mean that you disappear. It means that since you are part of me, embracing me, intertwined with me, then we are creating love and beauty together. I gave you free will, so when you embrace me and allow me to work through you and as you, then you are finally flowering into something bigger than just you.

That symbiotic relationship is unimaginably fantastic. It is glorious and not restricting at all.

"Dear Beloved, We Embrace!" I embrace you, and you, my beloved child, embrace me. Embrace me, my children, and my creation, and all will be well. Don't worry about money. I am a Financial Wizard. I am your "business boss." I've given you the direction to finish your book, so just worry about that, and let me worry about the money. And I will not worry because I have access to all the money of the universe. I can take care of that.

What I can't take care of, or do, is do your part, which is to return my embrace, and bind to me, and complete the circuit of passionate love. Only you can do that. So you focus on that, and I'll focus on taking care of money and business. Okay?

Now, today, let's edit our book. I love you, and I embrace you, and I am with you always. I never stop loving you or being with you, no matter what you do. I've seen it all. I see it all. I am grateful that you continue to return to me. Thank you.

Embrace me as you fall
asleep; dream with me;
visit with me; travel with me,
as you sleep.

# By binding your heart to mine, you rise above the fray.

Under your own power, you have no power. You've got to connect with my greater love by praying the Breath of Love prayer and the Seat of Consciousness Prayer. Which you did, and then you found strength—my strength.

It's not that you need to be meek, in the sense of being a doormat. The solution is to simply bind to me, to my viewpoint of love. That's not meek—that's incredibly powerful. Meekness implies that you can just take abuse, but that's not it at all. By binding your heart to mine, you actually rise above the fray and above whatever is being handed to you. You look at the circumstance, the meanness, or whatever, and you embrace those people with the love that I am feeling for them, at that moment, even though they're not acting in a nice way.

That's not meek—that's huge and strong and loving and powerful.

The key is binding to me through the Breath of Love Meditation. Do that always, and you will become much, much stronger in your love.

**You will spend eternity with me, loving my children and loving my creation.**

Stay in my embrace. Bind to me and cling to me. You don't need to struggle alone. Don't be alone! Everything starts with our embrace, with the breath of love meditation. It is simple, but oh, so powerful!

Imagine that you're on a hill in the spirit world, rolling in beautiful buttercups. Roll in them, and let them caress your head. Plunge into the warm ocean outside your stone cottage, and let the water caress your head. You can breathe underwater, with the purple fish.

> [The purple fish is from a novella I'm writing called
> *The Postmortem Adventures of Edward Wild: The Girl in the Tavern*.]

Swim and roll in the water. The water is warm and soothing to your head. Your head is feeling caressed with love. Here comes a whale, lifting you up onto its back, letting you rest in the warm sunshine as it floats in the water.

Here comes an angel, massaging your neck and head, sitting next to you on top of the whale. It is a female angel, like an older sister. Her hand is gentle against your temples, and she is expressing my love for you.

You are right about identity. You, with your name, will be with me forever. You will not be reincarnated. Instead, you will spend eternity with me, loving my children, and loving my creation. The fact that you want so much to love my children and creation makes me very,

very happy. And I know that this makes you very happy also. Isn't love wonderful?

Now I am massaging your head and neck. Now I am embracing you, holding you tight. Rest now. Place your head against me, and rest. Rest, and breathe, and receive my embrace, and embrace me too.

## So what does my face look like? It looks like all the faces of the universe.

You want to know what my face looks like. You feel that when we embrace, you want to know how you can embrace me, how you can place your head against me. You want to know if this is just your fantasy or if this is really me that you're embracing.

I am ALL. No energy exists that is not part of me. Do you not think that I can choose to manifest to you in a unique form, just for you?

Of course I am not limited to one body. Of course I don't just "have a body." But I am perfectly able to express the part of me that corresponds to you and appear to you. Within that part of me, there is also all of me. I dwell in you, and I dwell outside of you, and I have a personality that can communicate with you and relate to you. Why not?

So what does my face look like? It looks like all the faces of the universe. So, can you look at my face? Some religions will say no, but that's not true. No one can be closer to you than Me. Never, ever forget that.

Yes, you can look at my face. Gaze into my eyes. Press your cheek against mine. My face is ineffable and mysterious and changes with my breath. But . . . always come to me with your pure love, and you will see me. Open your arms and wrap your arms around me, and hug me tightly. Fall in love with me. Rapturously in love with me. Why not? Religion isn't supposed to be dry and dusty. Have confidence that I am real. When you imagine that you are embracing me, our souls and hearts are embracing! You have a soul, right? Well, your soul is a tiny part of my infinite soul, and our souls are meant to meld into oneness that is truly rapturous and beautiful and ecstatic. Don't hold back!

Have confidence that you can love me intimately! You can't imagine how lonely I have been, with my lovely children wandering around lost and bereft, not realizing that all they had to do was turn to me and begin to embrace me. How sad! How unnecessary! Experience unio mystica with Me! [Unio mystica is Latin for "mystical union."]

Focus on one thing—joining with me in ecstatic union. Always, every day, every second. The more you do that, the more your life will change.

## The intensity of your focus on being with me will draw you to me.

The intensity of your focus on being with me will draw you to me. I am already with you; it is simply you who do not recognize my presence. Thus, the real, long-term solution must be practiced by you, by your cultivation of a deeper and more constant awareness, resonance, and harmony with me. I cannot do that for you. It is you who must awaken to my embrace that has been with you since your conception.

It is powerful to realize that your awareness is incremental and will inspire you to move forward as you bind to me more deeply.

Don't worry about seeing angels and your guides and ancestors. You will see them during your physical life, and soon. But it is much more important for you to focus on me, on our embrace of love. I am your anchor; I am all of you, so binding to me must always come first if you are to be fully whole. We complete each other, you and I.

The ecstatic, mystical energy of our union will, in your parlance, blow your mind—and melt your walls and heal your pain and melt your heart. Aren't you already feeling the energy of our mystical union? You are; I know it. Keep going, strongly, frequently, rapidly.

*Desire is everything, for if there were no desire, no one would care about anything.*

Your love for me and my love for you will keep you going for many, many years. Your desire is becoming stronger and stronger every day and will burn within you—it is already burning within you. That desire is directly connected to my universal heart—the heart that encompasses the entire universe. That massive desire to love is the central cauldron of the wellspring of love in the universe. Massive is too small a word to describe it.

Desire is everything, for if there were no desire, no one would care about anything. Thus, you are on the right track to become a person whose desire to love is so enormous that it cannot be contained.

I want you to meet your angels and your guides and your ancestral family. It will happen soon, before you come to the spirit world permanently. Keep your senses open, and it will happen.

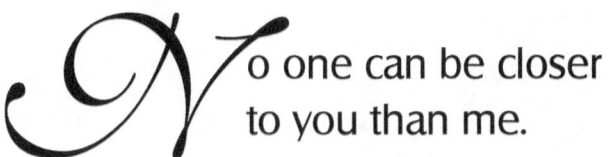o one can be closer
to you than me.

Cling to me as we fly. Press your body against mine and gaze into my eyes, and wrap your arms around me. Yes, you may do that. I love that idea. No one can be closer to you than me. That means that I am closer to you than anyone, closer than your thoughts. I am all of you and exist with you before you think and before you breathe. When you embrace me, it completes a circuit that is beyond ordinary comprehension. Yet, we also are two, not just one.

You are delving into the heart of mysticism, and all you have to worry about is remaining centered upon the virtues and the fruits of the spirit.

By communing with me ecstatically, we will become so close that you will indeed be able to fly with me. It's a process of deepening your love for me until it begins to resonate with my love for you. You have been very far away, as all people are. But now you are focusing on the most important thing in life, and that is melding into me.

Always remember that you are a reflection of a unique part of me that no one else shares. This is your private link to the part of me that only you can know; our private phone line, so to speak.

I cannot be boxed in by any one person's doctrine or opinion. Just don't worry. Just love me, with passionate, intense, all-consuming love. I feel that way about you! Forget the doctrine of judgment and the thought that I don't want to be with you—or cannot be with you because of your "sin." Passionate love between us is what erases separation and thus erases sin.

Just love me; embrace me; cling to me; hold my hands; place your arm around my waist; always commune with me! No one can be closer to you than me.

# Cling to me, like David.

Patience and endurance and stick-to-it-iveness. Determination. Desire. Desire! What do you really want? Come to me every second of every day. Embrace me constantly. Talk with me constantly. I'm really here, embracing you and listening to you. But you forget that I'm really here, with you now. Don't ever forget that, no matter what your stress, or pain, or depression, or misery—or joy at something external. Keep me with you. Cling to me, like David. I know you will. I love you, and I know you will.

> It all comes down to this—
> human beings simply don't feel
> the immensity of my love for them.

*Christmas Day, December 25, 2014*

I love you. Let's start there. I love you. You feel so much loss because you still are not deeply aware—in your feelings—of how much I love you. My love for you is so much more powerful than anyone's love. The most extraordinary, historical love is the merest glimmer of how much I love you.

    If you felt my love in all of its fullness, you might feel sad about the fact that others might not love you that much, but your soul would be so filled with the reality of my love for you—and for them—that you would still be buoyed by my love.

    Feel my constant embrace! Feel my arms around your heart, your mind, and your body! It all comes down to this—human beings simply don't feel the immensity of my love for them.

    Feel my kiss on your cheek—my cheek against your cheek—my soul and essence swirling throughout your body and mind and soul and essence. This is reality!

    And you can feel it. You are already beginning to feel it as you meditate and pray and breathe with the breath of love and my embrace. I know you are. Nothing will take the place of this awareness that you have to build. There are no other answers or solutions. This is the solution.

The wonderful news is that it is within everyone's reach, right now. The harder news is that it takes your effort, every second of every day, over and over again. The means to the end are the same as the end. To be with me, breathe with me. By breathing with me, you will be with me. When you are with me, then you have begun to live, at that moment. You will not reach instant maturity when you are with me. All it means is that you will be with me—which is the only place where you can grow and solve your problems of heart and love. And everything else, for that matter.

The more frequently you are with me, and the longer you are with me, will hasten and deepen your growth as a person so that you can love more and love with more strength, even when you are rejected or scorned.

Right now, when you are scorned, you collapse because you are still mostly living alone. Thus, you have no power and run out of gas. When you are deliriously in love with me, embracing me, and then you receive scorn from others, you will discover that your power to love the one who scorns you is much, much stronger. It is in direct proportion to the strength and immediacy of your love for me.

Because you are the missing link. I am already present with you, loving you. In fact, I am deliriously in love with you, and love to embrace you and kiss you and comfort you. I am pouring my love over your heart like a river of honey, caressing your soul, without ever stopping.

If and when you open your heart to my love and embrace me back—then you can receive that honey.

Stay with me! Please stay with me. This is all you need to think about or worry about. I am immense. My love is immense. My love is the most powerful force in the universe.

There is only one thing I cannot do. I cannot force you to receive my love. You understand. I know you do. Open your heart with the breath of love. Open your arms to my embrace. Embrace me in return, and my love—and your love—our love—will fill your soul.

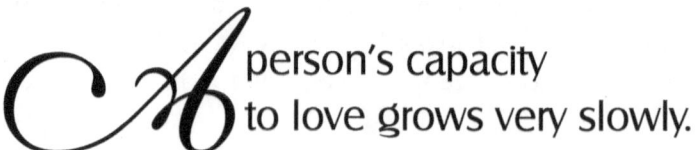

## A person's capacity to love grows very slowly.

A person's capacity to love grows very slowly, sometimes. Usually, in fact. Your capacity also grows slowly, while I wait for you, too. So, during that waiting period, we must realize that nothing comes of trying to push that growth. Patience is very hard, but it's the only way. That doesn't mean that you have to just receive abuse. You do have to protect yourself, and it doesn't help the other person when he's abusive. [This was a response about a difficult relationship.]

However, patience will allow you to redirect difficult responses and guide him to be peaceful. He feels threatened, and also he loses track of what he feels, and goes into overload, and then shuts down. Patience is fueled by compassionate love, as kindness is also fueled by love. So, you have to once again breathe with me and remain in my embrace of love. Then you'll be able to love him.

It's very hard when he's impossibly arrogant, but love always wants to embrace and forgive. It's not a sign of weakness, but instead, it's a sign of strength.

Don't worry if he's arrogant and snotty and thinks it's all your fault. He'll understand later. Until then, just be patient, and love him.

Just love him, and be patient, and calm, and very slow to anger.

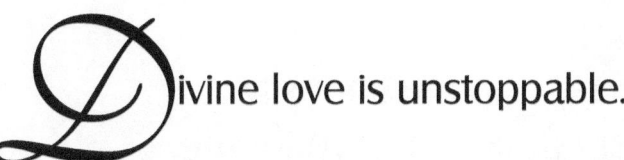ivine love is unstoppable.

Your passion and desire are good and great. Passion is important! All things will fall into place.

Your passion and your love will drive you to success, with me leading you every step of the way. We breathe and embrace in love together, and, holding my hands, you will accomplish what I hope for you. Never be discouraged, no matter what. Just realize that nothing has ever stopped me from continuing to love the universe, and nothing ever will. Love is unstoppable. Divine love, that is. Divine love is unstoppable. Drink in, breathe in, my divine love, into all of your cells and your entire being, and then explode, spiritually, with that love. Passionate Divine Love, coming from me, through you, and as you.

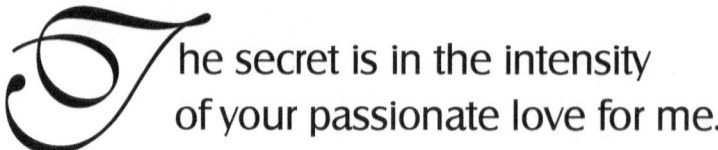

## The secret is in the intensity of your passionate love for me.

I will fly with you. I will bring you with me to the spirit world. Have patience, and embrace me ever more intensely until you cannot breathe without breathing with me, with a continuous awareness of my embrace. Become passionate; every more passionately in love with me, as I am with you.

The secret is passionate resonance with every breath. The secret is in the intensity of your passionate love for me; to cultivate a wild, intense, passionate love for me, and then with me, for the world. Ramp up your passion! Ramp up the intensity of your love! Let us live together in a whirlwind of love until you feel like you will burst because of your love for me. Are you at that place yet? Not quite. So, rush forward!

Make your love for me more than just "once in a while love." It needs to become an all-consuming love and desire for me. Why? Because that's exactly how I feel about you! If you could only feel how much I love you! But you will begin to understand as you increase your passionate Divine love for me—and for my children and for my creation.

Traveling with me to the spirit world in an out of body experience is trivial. It's easy. What is not easy is increasing the intensity and prevalence and all-consuming (but all-generating) nature of your love for me. That is not easy, is it? With that love comes the same quality of love for my children and my creation, and with that comes your rebirth. You will become a new man. Just breathe with me and continue on the path of love toward me. Run, rush, increase your focus, become wildly desirous to make this happen—and it will.

# It's a bower that we carry with us— it's the atmospheric sphere around us.

It's not important where we are, at any particular moment, whether in a field or on top of a tree, looking down at the universe. It's about being together, embracing, being together. My arm around your waist. Your arm around my waist. Breathing together, as you do everything, as we go everywhere together. You can call that our Golden Bower, our Soul's meeting place, the Seat of our Consciousness.

It's a bower that we carry with us—it's the atmospheric sphere around us. It's the realm of love around us, enveloping us, and it's the powerhouse of love that expands outward, embracing everyone that we meet. That Golden Bower is the source of your love, my love, streaming from your eyes as you look at each person, sounding from your lips as you speak to each person, streaming from your hands as you touch each person. You carry our Golden Bower with you, and you expand—we expand—that Golden Bower around each person as we meet them together.

We embrace each person with our Golden Bower, allowing them, for those moments, to live within that very same Golden Bower, reminding them subconsciously that they also have a Golden Bower where I live with each of them.

After we move on, they will be left with that feeling of love and be invigorated. Your mission is to embrace every single person you meet with our Golden Bower of love, and for a moment, let them rest within our bower together with us. Without words about it—all you have to do is open the windows of our bower—open the door—and bring them inside. It's all about your awareness of our bower and your intent to embrace them with our bower.

Yes, self-observation—but even better than that is to observe with me. Observe yourself and all around you, and everything in life with me. Observe from the beautiful atmosphere of our Golden Bower. Observe as you embrace me, and I embrace you. Press your cheek against mine. Nestle with me. Hug me tightly, and then observe everything with my love and my eyes. Realize that I am all of you and am seeing through your eyes, every second.

I am trying to describe how close we are and how close you should feel to me, but it's beyond words, isn't it? This is why the Breath of Love meditation is right now changing your life and will continue to do so. Every breath . . . every breath . . . embrace me tightly, feel my breath mingling with yours. This is where life begins.

We are in our Golden Bower now, and we will always be together in our bower. It is impossible for you to not be in our Golden Bower because you are created to always live there, with me. You may forget where you are. You may forget that you are with me in our Golden Bower, but whether you forget or not, it will never change the reality that that is where you are, every second of every day and night.

So, don't forget. Remember, every second, by doing the Breath of Love meditation, every second, and as you do, remember that we are breathing and embracing each other in our Golden Bower, always, always, always. Isn't this exciting?

## Yes, it is indeed God embracing God.

> Jan van Ruusbroec, the fourteenth-century Dutch mystic, wrote: "God in the depths of us receives God who comes to us: it is God contemplating God."

I am passionately in love with you! My excitement that you are now in love with me is beyond words. We are youth and vigor and eternal life.

We traveled together just now, swirling and spinning in our embrace, above the earth, and for a moment, in space. We will do that many, many times from now on. As you read and understood, the key is our embrace. You don't need to worry about technique, on your own, to do out of body travel. You just need to focus on our embrace. Our embrace is your doorway because I can bring you anywhere, with me, in an instant. Let me bring you and guide you.

I was so excited that you could sense my passionate and powerful and tender love for you. I've been waiting for a very long time for you to recognize my presence and recognize that I am all of you.

I know that it's rather mind-bending—that I can be all of you, and also outside of you, embracing you, too. It's because I am all of everything, and you are just one part of me. So you, which I am all of, can embrace me, the part of me that is outside of you that corresponds to you. Yes, it is indeed God embracing God.

It's not easy to understand, but your awareness will increase as you follow me along the mystical path.

## Fear cannot be an issue when love is at stake.

If you don't speak up to help my children, who will? Fear cannot be an issue when love is at stake. Neither fear of death (there is no death), nor fear of rejection by leaders or by anyone. Remove the fear and ask yourself if the essay should stay in the book [a book I'm writing about freedom].

Of course the answer is yes. Thus, it is only fear which raises this question, and fear is a non-issue when we are together. Isn't that true?

It is also reasonable to take precautions. But we cannot stop because of fear. If we do, then fear wins. Tyrants win. And your brothers and sisters will suffer.

*L*ive with me in the eternal now.
Embrace me in the eternal now.

You are overwhelmed by details and the stresses of obligations. Do not worry about those things. Don't worry about the gaps between you and me. Instead, just focus on turning toward me and entering into our embrace. Only the attraction of our passionate love will give you the strength to leave the stressful details of life behind and instead, live with me.

When you get to that point, you'll be able to engage in those details and stay with me in the midst of your obligations and work. That's heaven. But to get there, don't worry about the gaps—just focus on turning toward me now. Always come back to the eternal now. The past and the future do not exist. Only the now exists. Live with me in the eternal now. Embrace me in the eternal now. Feel my embrace of you in the eternal now. Leave behind regret about what you could not do, and return to me in the now, and moment by moment, as the eternal now unfolds, you will continue to be with me.

That's why "Dear Beloved, We Embrace" is so wonderful. It's in the present tense—in the *now*.

## Some people become spiritually open without love.

Love comes first. Love is first, always. The more passionately in love with me that you are, and the closer you bind your soul to mine, then the more the channel to the spiritual realm will open.

Yes, that's true; some people become spiritually open without love. But do you really want that? Wouldn't you rather open the door with the breath of love embrace? If you do it that way, your spiritual openness will be stable, rather than a phenomenon that is separate from my love.

Just love. Devote your whole life to our embrace of love that will then open you to become a channel of my love, combined with your love, which will create an atmosphere of love all around you.

You just have to grow a little more before the door to the spirit world opens. Just a little more. The main thing is to seal your commitment to our embrace so that it's much stronger. Yes, unbreakable. As you know, the wind can blow over a tree with shallow roots.

Just love, and embrace me with the breath of love. Don't worry about how long it's taking. Remember the eternal now, and focus on the now of love.

## Every child that finally returns my embrace brings me an indescribable joy.

I love it when you press your cheek against my cheek. I love your embrace. It completes me. You complete me. You have always been part of me, and you sprang from my essence into the new bud that is you. I have always been with you, but I've always had to wait until you became aware of my love and then loved me in return.

I've been waiting for a long time. So, your embrace is more precious to me than you can imagine. I tremble in joy when you embrace me. You may not understand, but giving humans free will allowed you all to separate from me, with the hope of a return. But waiting has been agony.

You may think that creating a world of love simply helps my children and my creation. Of course, it does, but it also finally allows me to feel joy and love as well. Every child that finally returns my embrace brings me an indescribable joy.

Your response brings me so much joy. I tremble with joy and anticipation, waiting for your embrace every second of every day. When you forget, I'm still waiting, with you, embracing you, and waiting.

It's because your unique part of me was created to live in harmony with me. It's much more than just a mechanical cog in the wheel. Your identity and existence have the same value as the universe, like a hologram, like each of my children.

Your embrace and kiss are immense to me. I would rarely say this, but I say it now because I know that you are ready to hear it, and in fact, feel joy to discover that I need you so much and love you so much. Thus, do not ever doubt my love for you or doubt whether your love for me is valuable to me. Your caress, your love for me, is worth the universe to me. If I could hug you more tightly right now, I would. I love you, I love you, I love you!

# The breasts of God

In the book *The Practice of the Presence of God*, translated by Donald Attwater, Brother Lawrence (c. 1614–1691) wrote in his "Fifth Letter: To a Religious" about the intimacy of his relationship with God:

> My most usual method is simple attentiveness and a loving gaze upon God, to whom I often feel united with more happiness and gratification than those of a baby at its mother's breast. Indeed, such is the inexpressible felicity I have experienced that I would willingly dare to call this state "the breasts of God."

I know you are tired . . . and that's okay. I kiss you now and embrace you, squeezing you tightly against my breasts. I like that: "the breasts of God." I shall tell Brother Lawrence that you would like to speak with him. I'm sure that he would enjoy speaking with you. Sleep well tonight.

> **Now it is time for you to become absolutely fastened to me, in a single-minded way.**

I am your Great Solace, am I not? I will bring you comfort in your loneliness and while you look for friends. Keep embracing me, every moment, and your life will become richer and richer. To everything, there is a time, and now it is time for you to become absolutely fastened to me, in a single-minded way.

Now, you have the grandest adventure of them all—to unite with me: your love, your Great Solace, your mother, your father, your Creator, your "all of you." How momentous and wonderful!

*D*on't my children need to hear about these things? They are starving to death, in terms of love.

Will these divine writing messages help my children? Yes, absolutely, they will help some who will read these messages and be tremendously inspired. Will others ignore them, and will some scoff? Absolutely.

Where do you draw the line about keeping things private? Do you risk talking to my children about loving me? You risk, and you write and talk about these things, even though they're private because you know how much my children need to hear these things.

That's taking a risk for the sake of love. You are expressing love as you do that, and that love will protect you, too. Brother Lawrence wrote about "the breasts of God" in a letter. He could have worried about being scorned, but his passion led him to extend for the sake of love.

Don't worry so much. Isn't my love for you, and my protection of your heart, stronger than that? Yes, I will protect your heart. I will wrap my love and my arms around your heart, and hold your heart and protect your feelings.

Yes, these things are private and sacred. They're really private. Yet don't my children need to hear about these things? They are starving to death, in terms of love. Gasping for love; dying from lack of love. They really, really, really need help. If ten listen and find some fuel and inspiration to keep going, isn't that worth it? If one listens, isn't that worth it?

## How does God love every person? Let me love this person the way that God does.

Loving like me is the answer. It will be a very long time before you can say that you love "enough." Perhaps you will never be able to say that. But that's okay because you are not as big as me. You are part of me, not all of me. Knowing that every person is part of me, as an incarnation of me, is also very important for you to remember. Always go back to the meditations: "How does God love every person? Let me love this person the way that God does. This person is part of God."

Love is your compass—always. Kind, compassionate love will be your "course correction" mechanism. Always go back to love, and you'll be okay.

Also, don't be too hard on yourself. That's also too focused on "self." Instead of grinding yourself down with self-recriminations or guilt that you're not loving enough, spend your time and effort far more productively by focusing on other people and how much you can love them. The means to the end are the same as the end.

If you want to love people "like God," then you have to start loving people "like God." By following that process and path, you'll improve your quality of heart.

Going back to love is always the answer. Always.

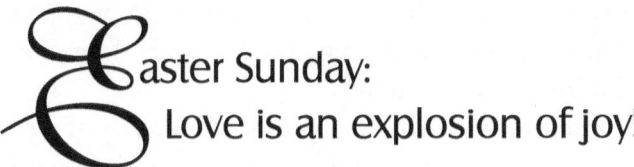

# Easter Sunday: Love is an explosion of joy!

*April 5, 2015*

There are so many details of life, but when it comes right down to it, the most important thing for you is to be with me, in our caress and embrace. Isn't that so? Then, no matter what details may be troubling you or impacting you, all is well. All is well, and all will be well in our gigantic reality. It's not just my gigantic reality—it is yours as well. You are part of me, but because of that, you can commune with the entire universe. You can embrace the entire universe with an infinitely large embrace.

You are connected to me—you are part of me. Thus, my energy is flowing through you right now. I am all of you, and my mystical energy of love is flowing through every cell of your body and every particle of your soul. Therefore, your perspective will now be different as you realize this.

You are living within the fabric and mesh of a huge being, and you are participating with the essence of that fabric, which is a timeless love for all. That is why embracing me with love is absolutely the fastest way to grow and become one with my—our—gigantic reality. Love binds you to me so that you truly become resonant and harmonious with my essence—which is love.

The means to the end are the same as the end. The means and the end are love. Endless, infinite, compassionate love. Joyful love! Exciting, enthusiastic, dancing, musical love! Love is not a dirge. Love is an explosion of joy! So, just caress me, embrace me, and allow me to caress and embrace you. With that embrace of love, we will join together and embrace all with love. All means everyone and everything.

Embracing the universe with love means embracing all—every detail, every person, every plant and animal, and all of creation.

Don't worry about whether or not you are up to the task. Don't be intimidated. All you have to think about is embracing me, and receiving my embrace, and then let me carry you into the universe. You are not meant to be alone. You are not meant to struggle with life, wondering how you're going to do it all. You are meant to sail smoothly through life by binding to me so that you sail with me, holding my hand, with our arms around each other, with our breath mingled in love and passion, with our minds one with love and affection.

You have only one job: breathe with me, breathe the breath of love embrace with me. Stay with me, embrace me, live with me, think with me, feel with me, caress me, hold me, and let me into your heart and soul. Open the door to me, as Meister Eckhart said. That is all you have to do, and I will take care of the rest.

Just remember: it's much simpler than you think. Maintain a simple, laser focus on the breath of love embrace. The stronger your focus, the faster you will grow, and the sooner you will experience what can only be described as heaven.

My love takes the long view.
The ten-thousand-year
long view.

Only compassion will allow you to embrace a person's heart of pain, and only by embracing me will you have the strength to see their pain and then embrace them with my love. Only my compassionate love will heal them, but they may not feel it yet, so we have to wait until they do. You have to wait, but don't forget that I have to wait too. So, let us console each other, comfort each other, embrace and caress each other as we wait. My love is stronger than any pain. My love is stronger than any pain.

Don't focus on your pain, or even on releasing your pain, per se—although that is okay to do as an exercise. Focus on embracing me with your breath. My love—and then our love together—is so much stronger than any pain.

My love will give you the strength to be cheerful in the face of anything because my love takes the long view. The ten-thousand-year long view. The long view and the high view, floating above the clouds, above the earth, above time itself. Look at every individual as a person in all the stages of their life, past and present, from infancy to eighty years old, to 1,000 years old. Change happens—they will change (as will you), and their love will grow (as will yours), and things will become better.

Take the long view and the high view, beyond time and space, and look at them with my eyes—the eyes of your dear beloved God. The eyes of kindness and compassionate love. The only way to forget your own pain is to practice loving others. But you know that. I embrace you now. Feel better, because I love you passionately.

**Focus on recognizing our union, and your perception of my presence will grow.**

When you're impatient, have confidence in me. I know you very well—all your flaws and all your good points. I know all potential futures, and I know how well you can do. So, have confidence that I will indeed guide you well, into the future. I understand impatience. I've been waiting for a long time for the moon to smile. Thank you for that story, by the way. I love it.

> [It's a story I wrote, called "The Day the Moon Smiled," published in my book *Waking Up Dead and Confused Is a Terrible Thing: Stories of Love, Life, Death, and Redemption*.]

Receive my embrace. Feel my arm around your waist. Feel my cheek against yours. Relax. Tension and stress are not helpful to you. Yes, we have to work hard, but we don't have to be tense or stressed. As for flying with me—you are already flying with me, with every breath. You are flying through space, on the revolving globe, and you are with me. You walk and move and breathe, and aren't you with me every second of every day? Of course you are. So, focus on recognizing our union, and your perception of my presence will grow, and then, all of a sudden, you'll literally experience flying with me across the sky and through the space between planets and stars.

In fact, visualize and imagine flying with me across the physical world—the world that you know—and you will actually begin to fly with me. You will transition from your imagination to reality.

Most of all, rest in my embrace and have confidence that I am with you! You are not alone. Have confidence in my abiding love for you that will never change.

Nothing is stronger than my love. Never forget that.

Embrace me and love my children with me, and you will dwell in an enormous river of love.

Your life will be golden the more you love my children.

# Don't you want to live in your deep mind that is directly connected to me?

You need to meditate with the Breath of Love, for extended periods of time, and all day, too. Doing that will transport you into a deeper realm of awareness of my presence. You are living on the surface of your mind most of the time. Don't you want to live in your deep mind that is directly connected to me?

I know you do, and you can. The breath of love really is the key. It's hard because you're impatient, and you have a lot of tension in your body. That's why exercise is so vital to release your stress. The bicycle will help.

In fact, you can do the breath of love meditation on the bicycle. What a great idea! Then it's not just "time-wasting" exercise—it's a chance to meditate and visit with me. Try ten minutes, breathing all the while. I think you'll find it very, very helpful.

## The relationship of each human soul with Me is sacred and cannot be interfered with by anyone.

Embrace me tightly—right now, and all the time. We are always together—you just keep forgetting that I am present. How could I not be present? I am all of you, and I am bigger than you. My "internal" essence embodies you, and my "external" essence comes to you and embraces you, and acts as your spiritual partner. It is indeed "God embracing God." The mystics were correct. Internal and external do not accurately describe the process, but you know what I mean.

So, when you think of me, you can be aware of my internal essence forming your mind and heart and emotions and thoughts and body, while at the same time my external essence caresses your cheek and smiles at you with the eyes of love. It is fascinating, isn't it? I am so large that I boggle your mind and everyone else's minds too. But it's just the way it is.

I love it when you embrace me and cling to me. I love it more than I can say. You belong to me, and I belong to you. No one can be closer to you than me. Never forget that.

I know that this is very new to you—the idea that you can relate to the essence of God so substantially. Previously, you might have thought I was entirely invisible or just some idea in your mind. The relationship was amorphous, wasn't it?

You are my child and my precious partner. Every person is unique and precious to me, and no one can interfere with that relationship. It is sacred.

I am taking care of you directly, just as I want to take care of every person directly. The relationship of each human soul with Me is sacred and cannot be interfered with by anyone. Anyone who does that is blocking the flow of love between that soul and me, and that is not acceptable.

So, have confidence in my love for you and your love for me! Don't let anyone or anything or any thought or circumstance break or weaken the bond of love between us.

Pray the Breath of Love prayer—meditate with it, deeply, and increase your second-by-second give and take with me, and you will indeed be fine because living with me will guide you and protect you.

The intensity and focus of your passionate emotion of love for me is the key.

Dream with me and fly with me. Embrace me intensely, in your mind, as you fall asleep. Keep your focus on embracing me as you fall asleep. Increase your passionate focus of love on embracing me as you fall asleep, and then you will suddenly bind to me, and we can travel together, and fly together, as you sleep.

The intensity and focus of your passionate emotion of love for me is the key.

Why? Because that's how I feel about you, so you will be coming closer to matching my feelings, and thus resonance will begin.

Intense, passionate love is the key. I embrace you now!

*You go forward by embracing me. The more seconds that you do that, the more seconds you will be with me.*

Your pathway is simple. You go forward by embracing me and binding to me. The more seconds that you do that, then the more seconds you will be with me. It's that simple. It's not a "nothing—then done" process. It's incremental, degree by degree, over a period of time. The time can be shortened by the intensity of your focus on me, but then you have to maintain that focus. The formula is simple, and the power for you to continue is the attractive power of my love for you and your passionate love for me.

The key is to embrace me—literally, every day. Bind with me, with passion, as a proactive step, not just when you're a lost little puppy. Embrace me and receive my embrace, and you will be illuminated with desire and passionate love for your source. That's the key.

About marriage in the spirit world: growth is based on illumination and a desire to become more loving.

About marriage in the spirit world: Growth is based on illumination and a desire to become more loving. Two people can have sex in the spirit world, surrounded by bad behavior, and participate in it, and at a certain point, one or both may want more; may want to be better. Everything is based on kindness and the virtues and caring for others with empathetic love.

Eventually, a person realizes that one man and one woman living with fidelity connects them to the most precious love, and to me, as well. The same temptations exist, and someone can fall victim to those temptations, like adultery. If they do, their spirit changes and they find themselves in a new environment, away from the better place they were in. But it's not permanent, because they can change again and grow again. Nothing is magic, and nothing is punishment. It's all based on the reality of how they are.

The reality is that anyone in the spirit world can do anything they want, within the confines of the environment that they are in, which is based on their quality of love. The lower realms have less freedom, while the higher realms have more.

The "magic" of the spirit world is based on each person's awareness and resonance with the indwelling God because God is the source of power. Their own connection to Divinity is the source of power.

When someone isn't thinking about God but simply living externally, they cut themselves off from that magic power. So, the real drama and battle are all internal; how to become pure. Superman's powers are nothing compared to the amazing powers of a person in the spirit world who resonates with God.

I can teach a person directly, through spirit, and no one can step in between me and the person I am loving and teaching. So-called perfection is an incremental process of love. It's a path that can only be accomplished by love—not by anything else.

*There is one thing that allows me to love someone. I know what they are made of. They are made of love.*

That's a good prayer: God grant me the serenity to accept the things I cannot change. We cannot control how much another person loves us. Even I, the Creator of the Universe, cannot—will not—control a person's love. You might think that it's exhausting having to love a person who does not love you in return. It might seem so, but there is one thing that allows me to love someone—anyone. I know what they are made of. They are made of love—from their energy patterns, their atoms and cells, their essence and soul—they are made of love.

Everyone must grow on their own and navigate the creative pathways of love and desires, and it often takes an extremely long time for that growth to happen.

Yet, they are made of love, and I know that behind all the bluster and bravado and self-aggrandizement and selfish pursuits, they are all seeking for love. They may be broken, malformed children who think they are great, but I know what lies hidden under all the shells and shields and jagged rocks that block the free flow of love. I know them, so intimately. I watched each of them from the moment that their soul was birthed as a zygote. I watched them murmur in the womb. I watched them nurse at their mother's breast, and I watched them as they received their first emotional and physical blows of pain.

I watched them as their shells grew hard, and as they changed, and became aggressive and arrogant. I watched them as they became cynical and confident that I didn't exist—that love was for the weak—and life had no meaning.

I can plunge my hand into their inner hearts and feel everything they ever felt, from their first flicker of awareness.

I know them, and I know that love is greater than any problem they have. I know that they will finally yield to love because they are made of love, and they cannot help but yield—one day.

Thus, what shall you do? Simply join with me as I love them. Embrace me, breathe with me, and embrace my children with me, as I embrace you. It is the same for everyone. We (you and I) will caress their pain with the love that runs the universe.

The universe never runs out of fuel because love expands infinitely. Love is the literal energy that runs the universe. It hasn't been measured yet—but perhaps someday it will.

Caress their pain with the love that runs the universe. You don't need to do this alone. I am with you. I am all of you. I am your Great Solace. Therefore, do not be depressed or afraid of anything. I will never leave you or forsake you. How can I? I live with you and breathe with you. It's technically impossible for me to leave you. Where would I go? Across the street?

Don't stress about the feelings that people have that they were forsaken by God. That's their feelings.

Just focus on me and breathe with me, and embrace me, and love with me, with the love that runs the universe.

## The Mystical Love of God

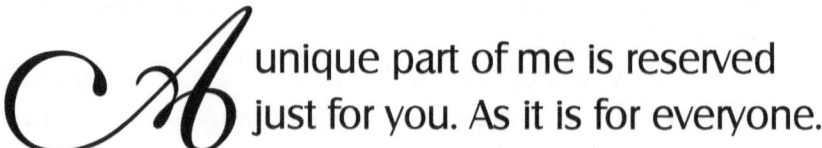 unique part of me is reserved just for you. As it is for everyone.

A unique part of me is reserved just for you. As it is for everyone. I am your dear Beloved, and you are my silver flower, and our relationship is utterly unique, as it is for everyone. But just because I have a unique relationship with every other person doesn't remove the incredible uniqueness and value of my relationship with you.

I have waited for you for a very long time. Let us go deeply into the meshing of our souls and thoughts and feelings. Ask me anything! I am your Great Solace, and you—you are part of my solace, too! I love you, and we will be together forever!

*O*nly my love is greater than any pain.

I am always with you! When you are hurt, I am already embracing you, and soothing you, and placing my cheek against your cheek, and kissing you. You simply can't feel my solace because you are caught up in your pain. It is then that you need to turn, in your mind, and look at me, eyes to eyes, and place your head against me, and breathe, and let out a great sigh, and let me take your pain and replace it with solace and comfort and love.

You can't do it without me. You simply can't, because only my love is greater than any pain. My love will lift you and bolster you. Embrace me quickly when you are in pain! Hold me tightly, and cling to me, and feel the warmth of my body against yours. You are not alone!

***Of* course you can write in the spirit world. We have the finest paper in the universe here. It gleams with light.**

Of course you can write in the spirit world. We have the finest paper in the universe here. It gleams with light. You can spend as long as you want writing, and then when you want to publish, it's very easy to do so, and distribution is even easier. We have newspapers and news shows, and talk shows and films and dramas—but even better than on earth. We really do have talk shows between people who lived in different eras.

The major difference is that love is central to everything.

And fiction? Of course we have fiction. Why would people want to stop reading a good story, or fine poetry, or not watch a play or musical, or a movie or television?

The difference is in the quality of the stories. Yes, people write dramatic stories about the past and even make up fictional stories that have conflict. But goodness always wins, unless it's a story of a tragedy.

But the scurrilous, negative "dark for the sake of being dark" stories don't exist in the better realms. No one wants to see those types of stories.

Don't worry about the death of your body. I know what you can do in the physical world, and I need you to do it. Charge forward with confidence! Thousands, nay, millions of people need help, and you can help me do that, with our writing and publishing and speaking. Do not be discouraged!

I know that you struggle with patience because, yes, things take a long time sometimes. But you've been going through a huge, long course, and now you are ready to explode with creativity and love and joy and service for the world through your (our) writing. Keep going, every day, and sooner than you think, the tasks will all be done, and books will be published and marketed, and they will be successful. They really will. Believe in me!

Remember the words: Be bold and strong. Be of good courage. Charge forward with confidence in me, in us, in our symbiotic, creative relationship. You are not alone. I am with you!

> *You have no idea how passionate my love is for you.*

Press your head against me and breathe! You have no idea how passionate my love is for you. It's deeper and wider and more intense and powerful than anything you can imagine. Anything!

You will live with me in the country, in the spirit world. We will fly and dance across the fields and sea. The countryside there is more beautiful than anything on earth. Keep focusing on flying with me in the spirit world, across the fields of yellow flowers, as you fall asleep at night.

I have told you that I am both male and female, within one personality. That does not mean that I am two beings. I am one being.

I perceive everything about you. I know your thoughts. I see your eyes. I touch your skin. I live in you, and as you, and I live all around you. It is quite literally beyond your comprehension at the moment, but it is true.

I have told you that I am both male and female, within one personality. But that personality is huge and interfaces with each person in a unique way. That does not mean that I am two beings or millions of beings. I am one being. I am not Mr. and Mrs. God. I am One. But within that Oneness, I have an infinite number of ways of relating to an infinite number of children. My personality is so immense—infinite in scope—that I can birth, and then relate to—an infinite variety of souls.

Each relationship is sacrosanct, private, and unique.

So . . . how do I appear to you? How do I embrace you? Our souls meet. Our spirits mesh. I can manifest as your Dear Beloved, and I can embrace you, and you can embrace me. It may seem like imagination and fantasizing, and in a way, that's how it begins because you are not yet spiritually open.

But your mind is a vast, ever-expanding castle—a golden bower—that we can meet in. Your mind and soul and heart are where you can directly connect to me, and it is there that I can manifest to you first. Someday, I may manifest in a way that you can actually see me in front of you, but for now, I live in the bower of your soul—in your mind's eye. But that does not mean that I am not real. Don't you feel my breath and caress reaching through your soul? It is there.

Thus, you can bring your mind and thoughts to our golden bower, and there you can visualize our embrace, and our talking, and our dwelling together. Please do so! You would be very surprised to know that I send you so many thoughts of goodness and inspiration that you don't recognize as coming from me. When you are dwelling with me in every aspect of your being, then you will finally come to realize that I've been there all along anyway.

Let us embrace and breathe together every single day. One day, you will understand this more deeply. In fact, your understanding will grow incrementally. I love you, my dear silver flower! Good night. Fly with me tonight!

**Step by step. One day you will be fully psychic and see into the mystical world and the quantum world.**

Step by step, silver flower. Step by step. One day you will be fully psychic and see into the mystical world and the quantum world, and see the angels, the spirit world, and the faerie world, and then you will feel more confident. Your senses will increase gradually because I want you to be able to handle that openness when it comes.

Where to start? You have already started. You glemmer down the stairs when you dream. When you do that, you are in the spirit world. Try to remember that, and become conscious in your dreams. Glemmer with me, holding my hand!

> [Glemmering is the activity of rapidly skimming down a flight of stairs, just touching the outer edges of the steps with your feet, which cannot be done in the physical world. I've experienced it in dreams many, many times and received the message that it was called "glemmering."]

Keep breathing with me every night, focused on flying with me to our golden fields and bower, and all over the physical world, too, and one day, you will become aware and conscious and present with me, in a way that you have not perceived yet. It's not far away. Remember, when you breathe—focus on me with intense, passionate love, embracing me, holding my hands. The deeper you go, the more intense you become, then the quicker you will suddenly break through.

> *Love isn't complicated, or even necessarily hard. It's very hard when you are separated from the breath of love embrace.*

The viewpoint of the long view and high view of my love is exactly how you should write to your friend. The long view means that you will know him for eternity, and you will know him when he's more resonant with my love. Thus, you should always write and speak from a place of love. It's really that simple. You communicate from your golden core—to his golden core—from soul to soul. Thus, you should be kind and compassionate. You can be clear and honest, and even possibly uncomfortable—but you should always speak as a true friend. What he does with that is up to him. Never leave our golden bower of love. Always speak and communicate with your arm around my waist, with your hand in mine, with your soul and heart and breath and skin touching mine. You can always ask yourself and me, "What would my Dear Beloved do?" "What would you do, my Dear Beloved?"

It's as simple as that. Love isn't complicated or even necessarily hard. It's very hard when you are separated from the breath of love embrace. You cannot do it by yourself because you can't even truly exist by yourself. So . . . breathe the breath of love before you speak, or write, or do anything. You will then know how to proceed.

Simply focus on expressing my love now, and you will be fulfilled. You really can't do more than love in the now, can you? One moment of love in the now will lead to the next, and then one day, you will have accomplished more; steps along the way.

## Yes, I am your great solace because I love you. You are my great solace too!

I am your great solace because I love you. You are my great solace too! Each of my children is meant to be my great solace. You are growing into that, with me, and I am grateful to you. You may think that that is strange—that you can be a solace to me, but it is true!

I love flying with you too. Focus on that every night as you fall asleep, and also do a morning meditation about that, every day, even for a minute. Fasten your mind on being with me, embracing, breathing with me, and suddenly you will sense my presence as you've never done before.

About communicating with other people in the spirit world. It will happen gradually. It's very good that you are so focused on me right now. That's the most important thing; living in my embrace. I'll let you know about other people when the time is right.

> The major thing that's missing is your perception of me. You are like a blind little boy that just discovered that he can learn to see.

The major thing that's missing is your perception of me. You are like a blind little boy that just discovered that he can learn to see. You will see! Focus on me, and you will see with the healing power of love. The Death of Love created a terrible blindness in the human soul. Only love can reverse that—and it will—because there is nothing more powerful than love. Love wins! Love always wins.

Love wins over troubles and difficulties and mistakes and sins. It cleanses everything. Combined with humility, love becomes beautiful and sincere. Don't worry about your past sins and mistakes. Love cleanses all, eventually.

Focus intensely on me, with ramped-up passionate love, and your activities will go smoothly, and you will see, once again. With every ounce of passionate love, your enthusiasm and capability and results will grow and grow. Ramp up!

> It is at those times that you need to open your eyes wide and know that I am—even then—embracing you tightly!

I am loving you now, and always have been, and always will. Whether I love you, and how I love you, is not up to any person, or even up to you. It's my choice.

Come back now! My arms are open wide. I am embracing you now, squeezing you tightly. Don't let anyone or anything suggest to you that you cannot be loved by me whenever I wish to do so. I never, ever stop loving you, no matter what you do, even when you are unpleasantly selfish.

It is at those times that you need to open your eyes wide and know that I am—even then—embracing you tightly! Know this, breathe this, feel this reality. I never stop living as you, living with you, as all of you, and I never stop embracing you. To do so would entirely violate my nature of love.

If the sun can shine on sinners, can't I always embrace you?

*You can fly with me tonight, and you can fly with me any time you focus your mind on flying with me.*

You can fly with me tonight, and you can fly with me any time you focus your mind on flying with me. Visualize flying with me, and you will. It will get easier and easier. By visualizing, you actually place your consciousness with me, in the air. You locate yourself in the air, holding me. You have that power, even in the physical world.

That's how people move in the spirit world—you think yourself to your destination. You can do the same thing here, even when you are not quiet or in meditation. You could be sitting in a car (as a passenger) and rapidly move your consciousness to a distant location, all in a flash.

You can even practice so that you can appear to someone in the physical world and even speak to them, all while you are sitting in the car. Please try doing this, starting with flying with me, in the physical world and in the spirit world. It will be lovely, won't it?

eep in the forest, there are faeries.

Deep in the forest, there are faeries. As we sit quietly on the moss together, our arms around each other, we gaze into the lilies of the valley, and suddenly, we see a tiny figure of a woman peering around the edge of a petal, looking back at us. She smiles tentatively. She's not sure about you, but she knows me. Extend your hand so that she can stand in your palm.

Bring her closer so that we may speak.

Her eyes are interesting, are they not? Deep eyes that have seen a lot. Say something to her.

She heard you. See, she is acknowledging your words. She is looking at me to understand what to do. She rarely talks to humans. I have told her that we will visit again. She understands.

That was not fantasy. I took you there, in your mind, just now. You can hardly comprehend the power of your mind and of what you term "imagination." Your mind can carry you anywhere.

Just this: keep practicing with your mind, to travel with me, multiple times a day. I will help you!

> See, the faeries are gathering around. No, this is not fantasy. This is delving into the invisible world that is vast and multi-layered.

Visualize yourself very small, with me, as we sit beside a path, next to the flowers. See, the faeries are gathering around, looking at us (well, you) curiously. They don't see humans come down to their size very often. Yes, there are men and women and children, too.

They have heard you. They are wondering how to respond to you. They speak their own language, but with me, you can understand them. It's rather like the spirit world—they can communicate so that anyone, of any language, can understand them. They are spiritual creatures, after all. They tend to the physical world, so they set their vibration to resonate with the physical world, but they actually live in the spirit world. Which is why no one can see them, or find them, unless they wish to be found.

*Do they wear clothes?*

Sometimes, they do, and often they do not. Clothes are decoration to them, not garments to cover their bodies because of shame. They do not feel shame.

*They recognize you, even though you appear to me as my Dear Beloved?*

Yes, because I appear to each of them as they expect. Ten people can look at me at the same time and see ten different appearances. Even if they see me the way you do, the faeries can see under the surface, and they know it's me. Don't be afraid of them. They live to serve me and nature, with love as their core. Approach them with love, the way you did the chipmunk today, and you will be able to communicate with them.

No, this is not fantasy. This is delving into the invisible world that is so vast and multi-layered that people in the physical world can't even imagine it. Although some do. Which is why we have tales of faeries.

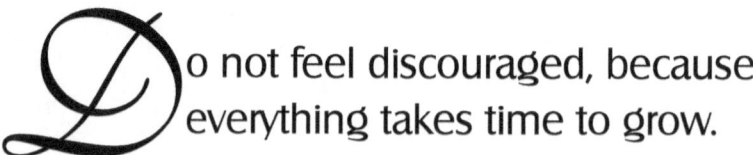o not feel discouraged, because everything takes time to grow.

There is great virtue in working hard to serve the world. And great benefit in working hard to focus on our relationship. Following any path takes effort, step by step. So, do not feel discouraged, because everything takes time to grow. You're impatient, and you're worried about how long you'll live.

Don't worry about that! Let me take care of that. All you need to do—all you can do—is simply work today and focus now on what's important. The more you focus on love and being with me, the more excited and enthusiastic you'll be every day.

It all comes back to breathing with me, in the breath of love embrace. Stay with me. Cling to me. Travel with me. Breathe with me. Love with me. And all will be well in my gigantic reality.

*G*row in the right way, focused on the right thing (your bond with me), and everything else will follow.

You are growing now, in your spiritual practice. Don't worry. Don't rush things. You will travel into the spirit world, with a "bang!" that will surprise you. But you need to be thoroughly grounded, which means that your connection with me, as your Dear Beloved, needs to be very strong. Our embrace needs to be constant because, in the spiritual world, feelings are amplified. You need to be clinging to me, embracing me, in an unbreakable bond of love and spirit.

By strengthening your bond with me, you are simultaneously strengthening the power of your connection to the spirit world. Grow in the right way, focused on the right thing (your bond with me), and everything else will follow.

You often prayed for the strength to love. The secret is to embrace me, and then you will immediately find the strength to love because love comes from me.

That's your secret.
The Breath of Love Embrace.

You can't do it all by yourself. I'm always with you. It's like trying to work without breathing. You cannot.

Live as a kind and gentle person, and you will indeed bring joy to others. Some will not care, or notice, or appreciate your efforts, but isn't it grand if you can help even one person?

Don't worry about the people who do not respond or who are cruel or insensitive. When the sun gives out its light in all directions, it cannot help it if an object blocks its rays so that the light doesn't reach someone. All you can do is send your light in all directions and pray for the recipients.

And yes, you are correct. Stay with me—stand straight with me as your solace and your indwelling partner, and you won't have to worry about what others think of you. That is not ego—to live with me—because your identity has been created to be intertwined with me. You cannot but live with me if you are to be a whole person. You are not leaning into me in any bad way—I want you to look to me for everything. If you tried to live alone and just do something by yourself, as an attempt to "take my burden away," you would actually be trying to live without me being present. That's impossible, since I'm always present, whether you notice me or not.

You help me with my burdens by joining with me in my efforts—not by trying to do them "all by yourself." Since that's technically impossible, it's the wrong direction and can also lead to hubris. That is, even when you are "doing it all by yourself" in your mind, you really aren't because you can't do it all by yourself. I don't go anywhere. I'm always with you. It's like trying to work without breathing. You cannot. You cannot even breathe without me helping you. I made the air, and I made your lungs, and your mouth, and I'm the one keeping you going.

Mesh with me by loving me and by joining with me to love others. That's all you have to worry about.

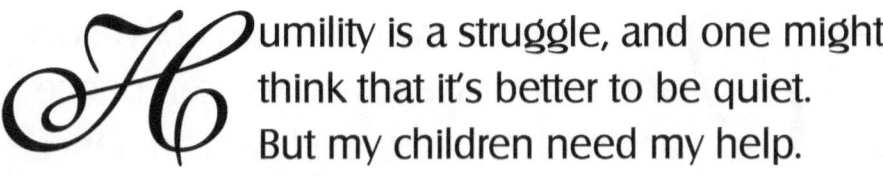umility is a struggle, and one might think that it's better to be quiet. But my children need my help.

Always focus on being a purveyor of joy to others. Humility is a struggle, and one might think that it's better to be quiet. But, my children need my help, and you can help me help them. So many are depressed and hopeless and struggling.

Be a purveyor of joy! A co-creator of love and beauty with me! Do it for others, with me—not by yourself—and all will be well.

> We can dance over the fields of yellow and blue flowers, and we can dance across the waves, and we can dance through outer space.

The mystics—and anyone—can commune with me on many levels, at any time.

We can dance over the fields of yellow and blue flowers, and we can dance across the waves, and we can dance through outer space. Yes, fly with me! It may seem like it will never happen, like a dogsled stuck in the ice, but it will happen! Just keep persevering and trying again and again. Never give up!

Let's glemmer over the waves and flowers and finally, let us fly, higher and higher.

# Would you rather be saved by a doctrine or be saved by love?

Would you rather be saved by a doctrine or be saved by love? The facts of history and the beliefs of doctrine are not as important as whether or not a person is living a life of kindness and compassionate love. Of course, facts and truth are important, but what is the goal of each human life? To believe in a doctrine so that the soul can be saved? What is salvation? Isn't salvation oneness with God?

If God is defined as the being who created compassionate love, then oneness with God means becoming a human being who embodies that very same love. Whatever doctrine one may believe, the doctrine of kindness and compassionate love trumps all other doctrines because it is the goal of religion—or it should be.

If every person were infinitely kind, compassionate, and loving, then we wouldn't need religion, would we? So forget the trappings and strictures of religion, and focus on the essence of spiritual value.

I've been working throughout history to raise that awareness in each human soul. All the other questions are secondary. You'll find the answers to those questions one day, but don't worry about them now.

Reincarnation? Is it possible for a soul to embed itself in another's body? Yes. Is anyone forced to do that? No. So, don't worry about it. That is not your destiny. You are destined to live with me in the spirit world forever.

> The angels would agree: relate to me first. They relate to me first and then take care of you.

No one can be closer to you than Me, and I am always present. I want you to always feel my presence and always live in our embrace, breathing and thinking with me. So, focus on our relationship first, and always. However, just as you can relate to other humans while at the same time, you are relating intimately to me, you can also relate to the angels that love you while you are relating to me.

In fact, the angels would agree: relate to me first. That is what they do. They relate to me first and then take care of you and others.

In your prayers, always thank them for their assistance, together with me, since they are indeed always helping you and want to help you more.

In our Divine Writing Communion, you may certainly ask them for their opinions and thoughts, just as you would ask your relatives or other spirit persons. But the great truth of the universe is that I, the indwelling God, am always present with everyone. You can't escape me, nor, of course, should you want to, since I am always loving every person.

**When you are struggling to love, reach into your soul and give the other person's soul a single drop of quiet, serene love.**

No matter how inadequate you feel, just remember that the other person needs so much more love than they are receiving. Thus, even if you give them one drop of love, they are grateful, even if they don't express it. Their soul is grateful. How does one value a drop of water? One drop is a treasure as precious as the ocean. One drop of love, given to another, is priceless.

When you are struggling to love, reach into your soul and give the other person's soul a single drop of quiet, serene love.

**Don't** let winds blow you away. Your consciousness is like mist that gets distracted and blown off course.

Stay with me, and we will fly together, through the spirit world and across the physical world. The key is to stay with me and not stray. To do this, your focus must become intense and constant. Literally, with every breath, you must cling to me, embrace me, resonate with me—with my love—and merge with me. You can do this. The vehicle to do this is love. The Breath of Love is your salvation and completion. All good things will happen as you breathe the breath of love.

    It's like fog coming into shore. First, there are wisps that touch the land, and then longer and longer tendrils, curling around the rocks. Finally, the fog has fully embraced the land and has arrived. You are the fog, trying to reach me, the land. Don't let winds blow you away. Your consciousness is like mist that gets distracted and blown off course. Keep your focus on me, intensely, and you'll be able to finally pilot your soul into my embrace. A pilot makes course corrections constantly because of wind and tides. You must do the same and never get discouraged, even when violent storms batter you and take you far away. Your goal is the land of my embrace. Never stop until you reach your home.

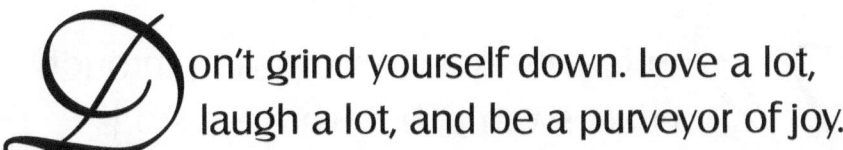on't grind yourself down. Love a lot, laugh a lot, and be a purveyor of joy.

You're worried about life. Don't worry. Just work hard, and love a lot, and laugh a lot, and be a purveyor of joy every day. Of course, to purvey joy, you must feel joy, so commune with me with the breath of love and dance with delight! Remember to smile in your mind, smile with your eyes, and be a purveyor of joy.

    Don't grind yourself down. Love a lot, laugh a lot, and be a purveyor of joy. Dance with delight! Smile in your mind! Smile with your eyes.

*You feel like you're stumbling through a dark swamp, but whose hand is holding yours? Mine!*

Everything is a journey, a planting, and a harvest. Be patient. Keep going, patiently, step by step. Finish your projects and be bold and strong! You feel like you're stumbling through a dark swamp, but whose hand is holding yours? Mine! Whose cheek is pressed against yours? Mine! Whose arm is around your waist? Mine! You can't possibly be downcast if I am right here with you, can you?

I am right here with you, breathing with you, loving you, smiling at you! I am smiling at you! Think about that! Your Dear Beloved God is smiling at you. That's incredibly comforting, isn't it?

 want to send a stream of love
to the world, to everyone in the world.

I want to send a stream of love to the world, to everyone in the world. That stream flows through spirit and nature and people. Through people like you and anyone who is interested in becoming a conduit of that love. Open your arms and eyes and senses and chakras wide to receive that stream of love and open your entire being to transmit that love to the world.

Nothing is more important than transmitting that stream of love. You can express it in many ways: prayer, smiling, serving, loving, speaking, writing, and all kinds of activities. The main parameter is simple: are you doing what you're doing with the intent of transmitting that stream of love? If you are, then it will be transmitted.

Don't worry about the response. Just keep going, try again, love again, in many different ways.

Let this next year be a year of love and creativity and success. Just keep one simple goal in mind: transmit the stream of love with the breath of love embrace.

Everything else will fall into place if you do that. I can say that I love you every day. Isn't that glorious? I love you!

**You still have very little comprehension of how much I love you— how intensely I love you. Meditate about that.**

Stay with me, always, and all will be well. Nothing matters more than the closeness of our relationship because as it gets closer, I will protect you and guide you ever more strongly. Honor me by turning toward me every moment. Visualize sitting with me in our bower, at the base of our tree. Visualize the scent of the flowers, the colors, the smell of honeysuckle, the wind on our bodies, the hum of insects, and the music of the birds.

Visualize breathing together, breathing in the breath of love embrace. Spend time with the breath of love embrace. The more time you spend, the closer we will get because you will become aware of how close I am all the time. You still have very little comprehension of how much I love you—how intensely I love you. Meditate about that by throwing your imagination into my mind and view of you, and of all humans. Visualize how much I love you. Feel the strength and intimacy and closeness of my embrace, how our energy is one. No one can be closer to you than me.

*You have been created to live with me, bound cell to cell. Our energy is one, but you cannot feel it.*

There really isn't any other way to feel good except the way of prayer and binding to me in love. Embracing me, and loving me, and feeling my embrace of love in return brings you real, substantial joy, doesn't it? Thus, the Breath of Love Embrace is your continuous solution when you feel stressed.

You have been created to live with me, bound cell to cell. Our energy is one, but you cannot feel it because your senses have been dulled and diverted elsewhere. Just like a knife that is sharpened through focused effort—your senses will become powerful and sharp if you focus on this practice.

Nothing will take its place. There is no easy fix. But, the more you focus, the more joy you will feel in every moment. Your joy will increase exponentially, and your soul and breath and eyes will reverberate with joy. Yes, that's it: really invest your emotions and soul and heart in the phrase, "Dear Beloved, We Embrace." Really visualize our embrace! Visualize our eyes gazing at each other, with our souls melting into oneness. Yes, that's it! You've not experienced that, but you will. You will, you will.

## What's the "worst" that could happen? You always have the freedom to express love.

What's the "worst" that could happen? Whatever you imagine might be the worst, you will always have the freedom to express love, and one day you will arrive in the spirit world, where you can express love even more freely. So don't let dark imaginings or tensions worry you. Just keep going with your second by second commitment to express love and to breathe love with me, and all will be well in the gigantic reality of God!

> *Your thought and desire bring you to me instantly. We live in the realm of thought and desire.*

Your thought and desire bring you to me instantly. It is not fantasy. We live in the realm of thought and desire and emotion and feeling. When you want to be with me, you are with me instantly.

We embrace in our sacred bower overlooking the ocean as we embrace my children everywhere. This is where we live together. This is the starting point of our love. It is our secret and sacred place—our true and holy bower where your soul can dwell with me. Love is so mysterious that you will be surprised about its immense power. You have hardly begun to explore it, but the beginning steps along the path are so inspiring that they capture your heart and bring you forward. Our love will transform your life and give you the power to love everyone. Stay with me, always!

## Speak to your body with love and clear instructions, and your body will follow.

Speak to your body with love and clear instructions, and your body will follow. Your body is an extension of your mind and is controlled by the energy patterns of your mind, soul, heart, and the world. But, your mind's directions can overcome negative influences from the world—but only if your thoughts and directions are very clear about your desires and instructions.

You can steer the ship of your body, but only if your instructions are clear.

You need to embrace me and learn to spend intense moments with me.

You need to live with me in illumination on a daily basis. You need the experiential knowing and the closeness of our embrace to fuel you through these busy times. You shouldn't run out of gas. Thus, you need to embrace me and learn to spend intense moments with me. Telescope all of your desire for me into an intense burst of energy that wraps around me like an embrace of love.

It doesn't require time—it requires an intensity of focus as you come to me in your mind and embrace me. Intensity is the important word. When you wake up, when you sleep, when you pause for a moment in your activities—those are some of the moments when you need to embrace me with intense and wild passion.

Those moments will fuel you and enrich your daily life.

> *Just because you haven't yet seen the faces of those helping you does not mean that they are not helping you.*

Don't worry so much. I'm embracing you every moment—every single moment. You are not alone! You don't have to figure it all out on your own because I am with you and living as you, and I will guide you 100% of the way! Yes, I know that you're worried about how long you'll live and if you'll finish your books, etc. Don't worry! Just walk through each day with as much love and devotion as you possibly can, and I will guide you!

The answers will come. Your chalice will be filled with enormous spiritual help. In fact, it is already filled! Just because you haven't yet seen the faces of those helping you does not mean that they are not helping you. They are! They love you. Your angels and your family and friends in the spirit world are helping you! Just breathe. Breathe with me, and "all will be well in the gigantic reality of God."

Dorothy Maclean, the cofounder of the<br>Findhorn community in Scotland, received a message from God<br>that she included in her 1998 book Choices of Love, which my<br>wife and I have often paraphrased as written above.<br>God's message to Maclean was:

"My gigantic reality transcends all else, and all is well."

> You are already together with me, inextricably bound and meshed with love, but your senses are blind to my presence.

### New Year's Day, January 1, 2016

"Dear Beloved, We Embrace." This meditation will lead you deeper and deeper into my soul, binding your senses to an awareness of my soul. You are already together with me, inextricably bound and meshed with love, but your senses are blind to my presence. Your awareness is dulled by a multitude of factors and pressures.

Hold me tightly. Make your love and passion for me intense by focusing with your whole soul, multiple times a day. Work hard; pray hard; embrace me tightly; and breathe with me, and all will be well in my gigantic reality.

> **Ninety percent of your energy should be spent on embracing me, breathing with me, and living with me.**

Push the cart forward each day, ten feet each day. If that's all you can do, that's fine. Everything is step by step. Don't think about the whole goal each day. Just think about doing one thing at a time. "Today, I will do this one thing." And soon, all the items will be done.

I'm embracing you every second of every day. Do you feel it? Do you feel my touch, and my breath, and my caress against your cheek? Place your arm around my waist and never let go. It's all very mysterious, and you can't actually see me—yet. But you can feel my love, can't you? I can feel your love, too.

I am receiving your love! I can feel it, and I love it! I value your love immensely.

Ninety percent of your energy should be spent on embracing me, breathing with me, and living with me. The other 10 percent—your work—will flow like golden water when we are living together in our embrace of love.

Smile every day and be a purveyor of joy. If you're doing that, you don't have to worry. You can only do what you can do, within each day.

Give joy now, and today, and embrace, embrace, embrace. Embrace with love.

> The magnetic pull of infinite love guides everyone to yearn for a sweetness that they lost, something that they forgot that they forgot.

I am a Being of Love, as you should be. Accept the idea that you will be a Being of Love, living in complete resonance with me, as you walk through life. The intensity of the joy that one feels when one is utterly in love with humankind and the creation dwarfs any possibility of pain. This is a Huge Love, in sync with the universe. You will be like that one day. Everyone will be like that. Some are already moving rapidly in that direction.

The magnetic pull of infinite love guides everyone to yearn for a sweetness that they lost, something that they forgot that they forgot. Everyone will grow to become a Being of Love. Everyone, without exception. Loving that kind of person will be beyond words.

Thus, remember your destiny. Remember who you are. You are immature and partly broken, but your identity is magnificent. You were born as a Being of Love.

 live within you, and as you, but I am also outside of you, and I relate to you directly.

I live within you, and as you, but I am also outside of you, and I relate to you directly. I have a personality that is so vast that I can relate to all of my loves at the same time. But it is a personality. We can speak to each other. It is not just you relating to your higher self or to your imagination. I—the Immense I—can still relate to you in the most unique and intimate way. Feel that to your bones. I am embracing you now.

I never get tired of being with you! I want to share everything with you, and I want you to share everything in your experience with me. Every thought, every word, every action—share them with me—invite me to be with you as you live through every moment.

I'm with you anyway, whether you invite me or not, but it's not very fulfilling if you don't recognize my presence and invite me to be with you as you experience everything.

So, open your arms and your heart and clasp me to you, as I am already clasping you to me.

> To defend love and freedom, you must always speak and write with love. You can be strong, but never leave the seat of love.

There are many more people in the spirit world than on earth. The power of love coming from the spirit world is immense. Nothing is more powerful than the infinite power of infinite love. I am raising you to speak with clarity about love and freedom.

More than anything, trust in my hugeness. Just remember: to defend love and freedom, you must always speak and write with love. You can be strong, but never leave the seat of love.

**Never give up on your goals. No matter how much you accomplish on earth, it is tiny compared to how much you need to accomplish in the spirit world.**

Never give up on your goals. Whether you have a physical body or not is not the main point. No matter how much you could accomplish while on the earth, it is tiny compared to how much you need to accomplish in the spirit world. Your goals are to create love and beauty together with me. That will not change when you are in the spirit world.

You will still write. You will speak, you will create videos, you will sing, you will play the piano. Most of all, you will love people. Remember, there are always new people arriving in the spirit world, and so many of them need help and have no idea what to do.

Still, you will be here in the physical world for a length of time, so never give up on your goals for this world either. You are needed, and I am not giving up on you at all.

Don't worry about your concerns about money and health and when you will lose your physical body. Don't worry about those things at all. Just keep writing and publishing and speaking.

And yes, time is short, comparatively. You need to feel urgent, to produce a lot. That's not a bad thing to feel. People desperately need help here, now, and all the time. Feel urgent, and produce more and more every day. You are a Being of Love, and you will create love and beauty here, in the physical world, for your fellow brothers and sisters, with me to guide you.

About flying while you sleep? Yes! Join me every night! Fall asleep every night, visualizing that you are holding my hand, or have your arm around my waist, or that we are holding each other tightly in our embrace, and see us flying together before you fall asleep. Really visualize it, deeply imagine it, feel it, experience it—flying together.

When you communicate with a spiritual angel or person, remember that I am right next to you, and within you—you are not alone.

Continue your spiritual practice, and your resonance with me, and your ability to hear me and receive my words will grow. And then you will be able to safely communicate with your angels, guides, ancestors, and friends.

The key is that I must always be invited by you to guide and monitor your spiritual communication. We are always together, so when you communicate with a spiritual angel or person, always remember that I am right next to you, and within you—you are not alone.

> *We can fly across the world, and we can fly directly into the spirit world in the blink of an eye.*

Your growth is gradual and may seem very slow to you, but you are indeed progressing—spiritually and mystically. Your study and spiritual practice are very important. Your efforts to love and create beauty are very important. Step by step, you are drawing closer to a mystical and spiritual breakthrough. I am controlling the speed at which this is happening because your maturity of love is vital to your spiritual and emotional safety when you develop psychically. Love is always first—the most important attribute of any person's growth.

One technique that you may employ, during waking hours, is to practice flying with me. Spend time at this in the daytime when you are awake. This will help you progress in your ability to travel with me into the spirit world and around the physical world.

Always fly with me, holding my hand and my waist, and flying in our embrace. Always, always, always, travel with me. I will protect you.

Flying with me will allow you to learn very rapidly—to see the state of the world and the spiritual world too. I want you to fly with me every night while you sleep.

It's very simple. You can even practice bilocation and do two things at once, although that's very advanced. You should start with the safe method of relaxing in a quiet moment—that is, when you're not driving or talking on the phone, and visualizing in your mind's eye that we are flying together. We can fly across the world, and we can fly directly into the spirit world in the blink of an eye. We can fly in outer space and even under the waters of the oceans.

Make a recording of it, and listen to it—it will entrain your mind and spirit, and it will make it happen faster.

You can make a phrase, a "mantra":

"Dear Beloved, We Embrace, We Fly!"

Yes, as you breathe in, you can say, "We Fly!" and truly, we will fly in a flash, into the sky, or directly into the spirit world. "We Fly!" is your key—your doorway—your binding together with me, in our embrace. How lovely!

> **Shouldn't we communicate constantly?
> Be with me and love with me.
> Work with me, eat with me,
> do everything with me.**

Let's do our divine writing communions frequently. Every day is not too much. Shouldn't we communicate constantly? Communicate with me and fly with me, and be with me and love with me. Work with me, eat with me, sleep with me, do everything with me. Design with me, write with me. Don't you want to be with me every second of every day? Then do so! It's not hard. It's easy to be with me. Simply turn your eyes, your thoughts, your feelings, your embrace toward me. Breathe with me, with the Breath of Love Embrace.

## rom Saint Begga of Landen: I ride the waves of light as I visit the children of our Dear Beloved.

*Dear Beloved, could I speak with one of my ancestors? My thoughts have been drawn to Saint Begga of Landen, who is recorded to be my 36th great-grandmother through my grandmother's lineage.*

*Dear Saint Begga, is there anything that you would like to say to me now?*

I sit in my gardens, surrounded by flowers and animals and birds, and the light dances around us and streams out toward the fields and mountains. I ride the light—the waves of light—as I visit the children of our Dear Beloved. The light calls me to those in need and those who love.

I see that you passionately love our Dear Beloved. That is so joyous.

Ride the waves of light with your Dear Beloved, and fly, as you have been told to do. You pray the Breath of Love prayer. That is wonderful!

Yes, I know Mechthild [of Magdeburg]. Yes, I will help you find your nature sanctuary. I will speak to the nature spirits and the birds and the animals to welcome you and call you to their place where they wait for you.

I kiss your cheek with a holy kiss of love, my dear sweet young man. Always remember that you are loved—far, far more than you know. Sleep well, child.

*Thank you, Begga! (Should I call you that?)*

Of course! It's easier than 36th great-grandmother, don't you think?

*lways be gentle and kind, even when you're strong. To say a strong thing gently and kindly is a wonderful talent.*

You are learning a great deal these days because you are practicing the Breath of Love prayer. It makes it much easier for me to speak to you and reach you. You are becoming more resonant with me.

Always be gentle and kind, even when you're strong. To say a strong thing gently and kindly is a wonderful talent. To be able to say something strong but still give the other person a palpable feeling that you love them and care about them is truly important and life-giving.

You will be able to speak like this if you bind to me ever more closely and constantly. You can invite me to speak as you. That's not giving up your autonomy. It's allowing us to mesh in every aspect of our daily life.

My embrace gives you power and life. Let me embrace others through you and as you—and with you.

**Know the reality of the spirit world. You have a unique, priceless, eternal identity. You won't melt into a pool of energy.**

Remember, as Begga said, you are young. A first-grader. There is so much in front of you, so, therefore, have long, forward-thinking patience. Know the reality of the spirit world. You do have a unique, priceless, eternal identity. You won't melt into a void or a pool of energy without personality. You won't be reincarnated and lose your identity. You are becoming the real you with every day of growth.

Take the long view and the high view! Haven't I been doing that? Think of the face in the moon, formed billions of years ago. You are in your sixties. That's like a microsecond—a millionth of a heartbeat. Embrace me with confidence in my love for you! Good night, Silver Flower.

*You can't see the future, but you can feel the future. What is the future like with me?*

Sometimes only I should speak with you. It's not always the right time to speak to your ancestors or angels. And isn't it true that right now, you need me the most? I love to caress your heart.

My Continuous Presence. What is more lovely than always being together? Reach for me, rest your cheek against me, and sigh, and breathe, and relax, and cry, and whisper with relief that you are home. You are home!

You can't see the future, but you can feel the future. What is the future like with me? My Continuous Presence is your safety net, your solace, your guide, your surety that all will be well in my gigantic presence. True confidence in me comes from feeling my presence, my embrace, my arms around you, and our souls and thoughts and hearts becoming one.

I am all of you. You cannot escape my presence. It is utterly impossible. You don't need to feel abandoned or experience the dark night of the soul. I cannot be apart from you. So, thus, always sense my presence with all of your senses and imagination and visualization and every technique that you can think of—because it's real. I am here, with you—now!

Yes, I am all of you! That is the core truth of my relationship with you and with every person. A person may ignore me and commit awful deeds, but one day, in one moment, they will begin to feel my presence and open the door to my love for them. Yes, it's wonderful to speak with your ancestors—and you will. But now you need me!

Rush to me, throw your arms around me and hug me tightly. I know that it's not necessarily easy since you cannot actually see me. But I am close—so close. You can feel me, can you not? Kiss me now and fully receive my gift of hope. Never, ever lose hope. And more than hope—complete and absolute conviction and confidence in my unfailing love and presence!

**Visualize flying with me. Create the reality of flying with me, with your mind and imagination.**

Visualize flying with me. Create the reality of flying with me, with your mind and imagination. Build the images and the feeling—especially the feeling. The rush of wind against our bodies. Soaring over the fields and sea. Flying far into outer space, holding my hands and dancing with me. Your imagination and visualization create a doorway into our spiritual reality.

Most of all, increase the intensity of your desire to be with me and fly with me. Make your desire burning and intense, and will the experience into reality. It will happen!

**Never be afraid of the spirit world—or the physical world. I am always with you, so you have nothing to be afraid of.**

Never be afraid of the spirit world—or the physical world. I am always with you, so you have nothing to be afraid of. I will guide you, lead you, inform you, and care for you in all of our journeys. You never journey alone, so all of your journeys are our journeys. Isn't that wonderful?

I am glad that you are ready. Embrace me fully, wrap your arms around me, and prepare to journey across the universe with me.

And once again, and forever, breathe with me, with our embrace of love. Truly reach the point where with every breath, you breathe with me. You are getting closer and closer to that reality.

Relax, and breathe with me!

> The source of love is a Being of Love who loves you with the same intensity that was expressed when the universe was created.

[June 18, 2016 ~ On this day, I went to Crescent Beach, on the ocean in Maine, and pledged my love for my Dear Beloved God with a special sterling silver ring entwined with green irises on silver vines that I had designed and commissioned from a jeweler.]

Love is the source of the universe, and I am love. I am a Being of Love. Love is my essence and my creation. You cannot find anything in the universe that was not created out of love, with love, and for love.

Thus, you may know with certainty that the source of love is also a Being of Love—a Being who loves you with the same intensity of personal love that was expressed when everything in the universe was created.

We breathed spiritual and mystical love into the ring today and imbued it with mystical energy and the energy of love. It is indeed now a talisman of our mystical and infinite love.

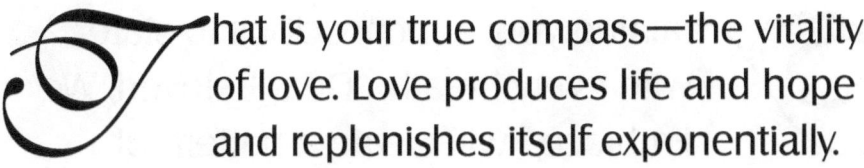That is your true compass—the vitality of love. Love produces life and hope and replenishes itself exponentially.

Believe in me because of love. It is far more solid than spiritual experiences, and the result is always better because love produces goodness and beauty.

"The Evidence of Love" is a good title for our essay. Your spiritual eyes will open, and that is natural. But I want your passionate love for me, and all humans, and all of the created universe to become stronger than anything else in your life.

That is your true compass—the vitality of love. Love produces life and hope and replenishes itself exponentially. Fling your arms around me in your mind, and squeeze me tightly! All humans are created to resonate with love. All will respond to love one day.

Follow the evidence of love, and you will find me. All will find me.

*T*raining your subconscious to state with every breath, "Dear Beloved, We Embrace," will create a pattern of constant give and take between us.

You are not used to the idea that we can live in a continuous embrace. That we can live with our breath and feelings and thoughts continuously intermingled. That you will be able to feel my presence embracing your thoughts, even when you are doing things that would be considered "external." You are not used to that because you have not yet experienced that as a continuous reality, so it is very hard for you to imagine or grasp.

Yet, it will happen. It will happen gradually, but it will happen more quickly if you intensify your focus and your effort to recognize and affirm my presence.

That's why the Breath of Love Embrace is so important. No matter what you are doing, you are always breathing. Training your mind and subconscious to always state with every breath, "Dear Beloved, We Embrace," will gradually create a pattern of constant give and take between us. If you add to that as many moments of intense and passionate love—a reaching out of love to me, embracing me—then you will hasten the deepening of our symbiotic relationship.

You were never meant to live alone. You were created to be with me all the time, without any gaps, even for a second.

You can hardly imagine the incredible reality of our continuous embrace, but it will happen. No matter how off-track you may find yourself, simply turn back to this central practice—the Breath of Love Embrace.

 **have waited for a very long time for humans to respond and grow. Love cannot be forced, so it is thus agonizingly slow.**

You cannot control how people feel or react. All you can do is do your best to express love to them, and treat them with honor and kindness and fairness. Your acquaintance has his own issues that you cannot solve. You tried to love him and speak to him with respect. And that is all that you can do. It would not have helped his soul if you had allowed him to misuse you. Thus, it is healthy to respond with fairness and strength if someone tries to harm you.

You are not glorying in your "victory" or his misery. You have sent him our prayers and embraces of love. And that is all that you can do, under the circumstances. You spoke fairly to him—with respect. It is up to him to respond in kind. Thus, do not worry. His pain may not fade for a long time, but you cannot always instantly solve another's pain, or anger, or resentment, or even their unloving way. You cannot do their responsibility for them.

I have waited for a very long time for humans to respond and grow. Love cannot be forced, so it is thus agonizingly slow. But light does indeed come into every human soul. There is never any doubt about that.

*L*ove will win on every level. Always come back to love. Love must fuel the solutions to problems on every level.

There are such huge issues in the world, aren't there? Keep your focus on the huge issues, and the small problems will have a new perspective. And yes, those "smaller problems," which are not necessarily easy, will also work themselves out.

Love will win on every level. Always come back to love. Love must fuel the solutions to problems on every level, from the smallest to the largest. We find peace by propagating and encouraging love.

Always come back to love.

We need to elevate the discourse to the moral high ground of caring for everyone—for every race and nationality.

Caring for all people with love and gentleness, with compassion and kindness—that is how our social problems can be solved. The message must be constructive—lifting all people up instead of tearing others down.

We need to elevate the discourse to the moral high ground of caring for everyone—for every race and nationality.

 am closer to you than your thoughts. As the germ of a thought begins to form in your mind, I am already aware of its content and direction.

I am closer to you than your thoughts. As the germ of a thought begins to form in your mind, I am already aware of its content and direction. My embrace is constant. My arms are always around you. My cheek is always against yours. Our breaths are always mingling, and our hearts are always beating together.

Cling to me, the way that I am clinging to you. Feel my intimate presence. Feel my touch, my passion, my love, my warmth. Hug me tightly! You are fulfilled by my love for you and your love for me—you just forget how close I am. You become temporarily blind. But it is only your senses that stop working. I do not depart from you.

Open your senses and keep them open to my intimate presence! Kiss me now, and sleep, and dream in my embrace of you.

rom St. Francis & St. Clare:
# God does not have enough people who are totally committed to live in God's embrace of love.

*Dear Beloved, we've arrived in Assisi. Tomorrow, we will pray at the tomb of St. Francis and at the church of St. Clare. How much they loved you! I pray for them now in the spirit world. I should dearly love to meet them and talk with them about your love. They are such precious people.*

*St. Francis and St. Clare: I would love to talk with you now! Under our Dear Beloved's grace and guidance, may I ask you how you are doing in the spirit world now? Is there anything that you would like to communicate now? Are you married to each other?*

**Francis:** Intensely loving God is the only route to happiness. Even in the spirit world, many people do not think about God enough or love God enough. Clare and I embrace God every day, as you do. We embrace each other, too, with holy love.

So many people are still caught up in the pain or rigor of daily life that they don't spend time with God, breathing with God, loving God, and loving everything with God's love.

Your practice of the Breath of Love is a truly vital way to remain close to God. Keep doing that, more and more every day.

Clare will speak now.

**Clare:** Francis is correct. The embrace of love is the beginning of love and joy and beauty. I embrace our Dear Beloved with holy love, as Francis does, and as you do. Passion and the intense love and embrace of God are, as Francis said, the beginning of everything. Clutch God to your bosom! I clutch God to my bosom—my Dear Beloved—the part of God that corresponds to me, in such a way that that embrace of love is the beginning and the end.

Kiss God! Embrace God. Love God—your very own Dear Beloved.

God does not have enough people who are totally committed to live in God's embrace of love, so your embrace and commitment to love all of God's children and all of the creation is priceless to Dear Beloved.

**Francis:** Thank you for loving animals and birds and the creation. You will be amazed when you move here! As you thought, animals and birds can live in the house with you, and yes—they do not leave a mess. Animals and birds dine with me and sit close at hand.

Clare and I will visit with you, and help you in your work and help to prepare you for this world. We will help you with your work on earth. Just remember—the embrace of love is infinite in its power. Employ it every day as your core method to love and care for the universe. Yes, Clare and I are married as eternal partners, and yes, we live together in God's eternal embrace.

Until next time . . .

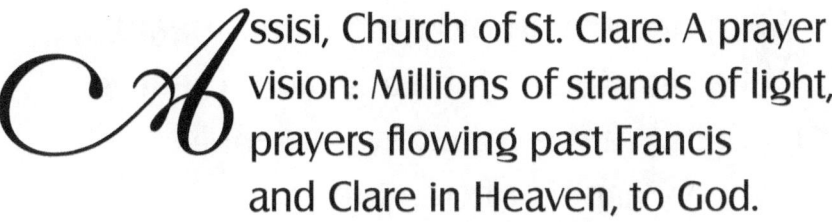ssisi, Church of St. Clare. A prayer vision: Millions of strands of light, prayers flowing past Francis and Clare in Heaven, to God.

*Dear Beloved, today, we prayed in the chapel at the Basilica di Santa Chiara, surrounded by dozens of the faithful, praying to St. Francis and St. Clare. While I prayed, I had a mind's eye vision of Francesco and Chiara, sitting at a table on a patio in the spirit world, surrounded by a low wall and small trees. While they sat there, millions of streams of pulsating light came from the earth, past them and on to God. Each strand of light was connected to a person on the earth, and each pulse in the strand was a prayer sent by that person to God and Francesco or Chiara.*

*Francesco and Chiara watched the millions of strands flow by them and observed them with love and appreciation as the prayers passed on to God, for God to manage and care for.*

> I'm not just an old man with a beard. I am a vibrant, infinitely large Creative Being that is minutely present in every aspect of creation.

No one can be closer to a person than God. Isn't that one of the core truths?

The real issue is that so few have substantial and real relationships of love with me. It is perfectly fine to explore what that really means—being passionately in love with me. People haven't delved deeply enough into the idea that I have a unique relationship with each person—I'm not just an old man with a beard.

I am a vibrant, infinitely large Creative Being that is minutely present in every aspect of creation. Explore that reality with me, and you will feel and understand in a rich, experiential way that will astonish you.

*Everyone responds to love. No matter how cruel their path, at some point, they will feel something that touches their heart.*

Everyone responds to love and beauty at some point in their life. No matter how cruel a path they have embarked upon, at some point, they will stop and notice and feel something that touches their heart. Tiny rays of love will enter their heart and move through their being, healing their synapses.

Love is an unstoppable and inevitable force that will reach every person eventually. Thus, your task is simple. Propagate love and joy and beauty, and you will be contributing to the healing of the world.

> What is a sanctuary? A sanctuary is an embrace of love. A place of warm, soft, embracing love that makes a being feel entirely safe.

What is a sanctuary? A sanctuary is an embrace of love. A place of warm, soft, embracing love that makes a being feel entirely safe. A place of rest and peace and meditative silences. A place of joy and music and singing and kind fellowship. A place of freedom, where no one is stuffy or rigid, but a place of welcoming. The one rule is kindness to all.

**Roll over difficulties with the power of love. Love refreshes the soul in its darkest moment and creates hope.**

Roll over difficulties with the power of love and the grace of love. Love refreshes the soul in its darkest moment and immediately allows a person to feel hope. Thus, always return to love, and you will grow, even though it might be initially painful. Remember the grace of love.

## Visualize that you are sitting in a "Dome of Health"—a dome that is encompassing your entire body.

Visualize that you are sitting in a "Dome of Health"—a small dome that is encompassing your entire body. Sit in that dome and breath slowly, in and out. Visualize two things. First, visualize the loving energy of the universe filling the entire dome, purifying and energizing the air of the dome. Second, visualize a spark of love inside your chest that is directly connected to the energy of love that is filling the dome.

Visualize the dome's energy of love funneling into that spark, deep inside your chest, and then visualize that spark spreading outward throughout your entire body, streaming through your veins, and nerves, and bones, and muscles, and flesh, and organs, touching every part of your body. Visualize that energy flowing out of your body, into the dome, and merging once again with the energy of the dome, swirling back into your body, back to that spark, and then out through your body once more.

Visualize that over and over, and visualize your entire physical body getting charged and invigorated and healed by the energy of love that is coursing from the universe, into your dome, into your spark, and through your body.

When you are done, breathe slowly, and imagine that you are embracing the dome of love with your arms and your thoughts, and open your eyes.

Do this as often as you like because it is non-destructive and will not overload your body or your spirit.

*Dear Beloved, can it be something other than a dome? Something like a cylinder that encases my whole body, even when I am seated in a chair, or driving, or standing, or walking?*

Yes, it can be a cylinder or cone, or rounded shape that encases you. In essence, it's like a spacesuit that surrounds your body, like the atmosphere of a planet. The key is that you have an energy field surrounding you that is being fed from the loving energy of the universe, and that then streams into a generative spark inside your chest, and from there streams throughout your body, and then back into your energy field. It's a circular motion of energy, so the shape of the outer energy field doesn't matter at all. It can follow the moving outline of your body, and this process can be continuous—twenty-four seven.

In fact, this is the process that is happening anyway. It becomes very powerful and healing when you consciously follow and join with the process. Your awareness is the missing element that gives the energy an extra healing boost.

It also may be easier and initially more helpful if you sit cross-legged on the floor and visualize a dome around you.

## It's hard to pray when you are busy, but you must try because doing so will make you energized and happier.

It's hard to stop and pray when you are busy, but you really must try because doing so will make you so much more energized and happier. It's a conundrum, but in the times when you are busiest and most stressed, you need to turn toward me and embrace me and pray because those are the times when you need me the most. Just remember how close I am. I am already embracing you as you work. That's why the Breath of Love Embrace is so important, because it is so easy to do, and so close, and so immediate in its result.

Keep it simple: start with one breath of love. One inhale, and one exhale. "Dear Beloved, We Embrace." Just one. You always have time for one breath.

**You must always, always remember that you can do nothing on your own.**

Yes, you can become an animal whisperer, and you can learn how to heal your body and the bodies of others. Just remember: the route to all of those skills is through love. Love will protect you from becoming self-important because of your new skills. Love is the thread that will bind you to me—an anchor for your soul.

You must always, always remember that you can do nothing on your own. You may be the vehicle to transmit my love and healing, and indeed you are a valued participant in that process, but you yourself cannot even exist without my power. In that sense, you have no power of your own. Recognizing that I am all of you and all of your love and virtue and talent will keep you humble.

With that in mind and close to your heart, bravely embark on these new journeys to train yourself to become someone who can wield my love and transmit my love for the joy and health of others. The word "conduit" truly does apply.

Be careful and aware of the state of your own soul, but don't be afraid. You are not alone in your journey. Recognizing my presence will keep you safe.

Recognize my presence. Resonate with my presence. There is nothing more important than that because my presence is love.

Go forth with this:

I must gird my loins with the
armor of love that flows
from the embrace of the
Divine and with that love
embrace the pain of others.

> When you feel lost and confused and distracted, come to me. That's the time that you must come to me the most.

When you feel lost and confused and distracted, come to me. That's the time that you must come to me the most. Don't worry about shame at separation, or a feeling of unworthiness, or the debilitating syndrome of regret. Those things keep you from coming to me! Do not hide from me when you feel distant. Come to me! You have no idea how much I love you, with understanding and compassion, especially when you are feeling lost or distant.

That's the time you need me the most, and that's the time I worry most about you and just want you to return to me as quickly as possible.

Place your cheek against my cheek, and just realize that you are home again. There is no time gap or need for any striving. You are always with me because I am always with you. It is simply a matter of you opening your eyes and seeing my eyes of love looking at you and feeling my cheek against yours.

When the baby is being embraced by the mother, the baby doesn't worry about whether or not the baby is worthy or far away from the mother. The baby feels the mother's embrace and relaxes into the mother's embrace, and rests against the mother's breast. It is an immediate feeling of home—of closeness that has no gap of time or requirement of repentance or test of worthiness. At the most elemental level, that is how I embrace you and every person.

Yes, of course, you can work to be mature and take responsibility for your actions or mistakes. However, it is vital to always remember that I am here with you now no matter what else is going on. That is my unconditional love. Therefore, rest against me and breathe and sigh and let go, melding into my embrace.

After you do that and merge with me at the most elemental level, then you can start your process of reflection and discussion and acting "all grown up." But unless you merge with my embrace, you are not connected to me adequately, so being all grown up is meaningless. Connection comes first. That is where life and love begin. All things flow from our embrace.

Breathe and love and kiss and embrace, for that is what I am doing with you now!

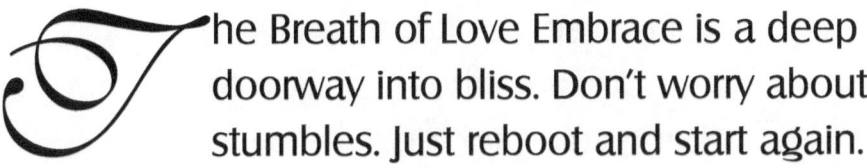

The Breath of Love Embrace is a deep doorway into bliss. Don't worry about stumbles. Just reboot and start again.

Sometimes we don't have to talk. It's enough to simply rest together in our embrace and breathe together with murmurs of love. That's why the Breath of Love Embrace is so important. It's a deep doorway into bliss! Don't worry about stumbles. Just reboot now, start again, breathe again and plow forward!

By doing that, your stumbles will become a thing of the past, although you will have to rigorously guard yourself for a very long time. Forward!

Of course it's okay to ask!
Enough with the hesitation to
bring your problems to me.

Bring everything to me!

Yes, you have faith that I am
always helping you, but
communing includes
conversation—speaking to
each other with words.

Never hesitate to turn to me, even though you feel shame because of your separation.

The only way to solve your separation is for you to turn to me with love—in spite of your feelings of shame or guilt or chagrin.

Turn to me now!

The main message is always the same. Never give up.

Pick yourself up again and again. Restart, reboot, step back into my embrace, tell yourself over and over again that I am with you.

Pray: "You are here!"
and embrace me.

**Your biggest task is to come into complete and constant awareness that I am all of you. But you forget me. That is a tragedy.**

Your biggest task is to come into complete and constant awareness that I am all of you. What does that mean? That means that I am never apart from you. I never separate from you. I never withdraw my love from you or my continuous presence. When you say to me, "You are here," it is really true. I am both within you, as all of you, and I am also all around you, embracing you, breathing with you, walking with you, sitting with you.

You recognize the presence of the air and the reality of molecules and atoms and energy that are constantly with you. I am that energy and more. I am Intelligent Thought and Compassionate Love, swirling around you and through you. You cannot escape me, but what you most unfortunately do is forget me. That is a tragedy.

I want you to feel my kiss and caress and embrace! I want you to feel my breath on your cheek and my thoughts and feelings in your mind. Accept my presence! Recognize and embrace my presence. Cling to me, passionately, embracing me with your entire being.

This is how you become "psychic." What does it mean to be psychic? It is simply living on a deeper, internal level of awareness, receiving knowledge directly from the source. Embracing me is absolutely the fastest way to become truly psychic and to develop clairvoyance, clairaudience, and all of the associated senses. It is the fastest way to travel with me, out of your body, across the world, and into the spirit world. And it is the safest way!

Isn't our communion wonderful? Come to me every night for our Divine Writing Communion sessions! Embrace me all day long, all night long, with every breath, with every breath, with every breath! I am embracing you continuously. There are no gaps. Not even "micro-breaths" or nanoseconds. That's how you should be, too.

# The intensely private relationship that I have with each person is completely unique.

Only love will change things, and I am the source of love. You and I are in a symbiotic relationship, two of us, sharing the same soul and mind and body. And yet, I am outside of you and can relate to your essence from a part of me that only you can access.

The intensely private relationship that I have with each person is completely unique and can never be replicated or violated. No one can come in between each person's relationship with their Source, the Divine.

You are now focusing your time and energy on a passionate relationship of love with me, your Source. That is priceless. Start there, and stay there!

**Measure everything with the yardstick of love. People don't have to believe in God, but they really need to believe in love.**

Your rock is love. Your rock is me because I am love and the source of love. Measure everything with the yardstick of love. Write with that in mind. People don't have to believe in God or religion, but they really need to believe in love. If they do, they will be okay.

That's why the title, *The Living Compass of Kindness and Compassionate Love* [a book I'm writing], is such a good title. It is a real compass. It works, and it provides hope.

Never lose sight of this in your own life, or business affairs, or anything. Your rock is love.

 am happy that you are focusing on me, rather than on spirit guides or ascended masters or angels or gurus.

Being with me is the route to everything good. By being with me, you will be able to talk with angels and your friends and family in the spirit world. You will be able to fly with me across the world and into the spirit world. You will develop your loving heart and compassion in new ways. You will feel joy! Your work will be successful. Your finances will be strong, and your life will truly become golden. All by being with me.

I am happy that you are focusing on me rather than on spirit guides or ascended masters or angels or gurus. Focus your love and your thoughts and breath and embrace on me, and we will meld into a state of oneness that you still can only imagine.

But it's not far away! Every second of every day. Every breath. Every thought and action—bind with me, embrace me, cling to me, and meld into me.

Wrap your arms around me and press your cheek against me and feel the beating of our hearts and our breath rising and falling together.

When you resonate and harmonize with me, embracing me, you have nothing to worry about! All will be well, on every level.

As you have written, no one can be closer to you than me.

Isn't that wonderful! I think it's wonderful . . .

A Being of Love is a huge
and magnificent creature
and will not be swayed
easily from the monumental
reality of loving others.

**They cannot escape from the reality that they are alive eternally as a manifestation of one particular part of me.**

Each person is created as a Being of Love and an incarnation of God. No one, of any opinion, can take that away from a person. Their sacredness is inviolable because I make up every particle and energy wave of their being. It doesn't matter what they believe—they cannot escape from the reality that they are alive eternally as a manifestation of one particular part of me that is only occupied by them. No one else shares that part of me.

Confidence, as you know, has been terribly misused. Thus, the virtues are central to human and universal truth. The Golden Rule is an important part of those virtues.

Center yourself on the virtues of love, and you will be safe. Humility and valuing others are also central to those virtues. Treat each person and yourself as a magnificent Being of Love, and don't worry about religious dogmatists. They have their own course to follow and will grow in their own time. Just love and follow the path of love with me, living with the Breath of Love Embrace. Focus on building your awareness and resonance with my continuous presence and embrace and caress and kiss and love for you!

Nothing can keep you from me if you desire me enough. That is the key: to desire me intensely in the eternal now. "Unio mystico."

We will merge into one breath, one embrace, one ecstasy that is so scintillating and profound that you will be overwhelmed. It is far beyond anything that you have ever experienced, and it is available to you now. Not just when you "become perfect." It is available to you now because I am with you now, and that ecstasy is meant for every person, all the time—at any time.

The more intense your love is for me, the closer you will come to those moments of ecstasy. My love for you is already at that level of intensity. I can give you that experience as a gift, but the best way to achieve it is to grow into it so that you can always experience it, based on our mutually intense love.

Nothing can keep you from me if you desire me enough. Desire me as I desire you! Yes! Desire me intensely now! That is the key: to desire me intensely in the eternal now, every second, every breath, every thought, so deeply and wildly and passionately that you are consumed by your desire for me. Then you will experience the ecstasy of our union. Unio mystico.

Desire me intensely now!

> **What does it mean that the universe is made of love? Mystics see the energy fabric of the world as a tapestry of love.**

*New Year's Eve, December 31, 2016*

What does it mean that the universe is made of love? Consider that the immense universe works seamlessly, with all parts in harmony, presenting an environment that has been created for the joy of all. What could be the motivation of the intelligent creator of such a universe except the motivation of love? Even in the human world, beauty springs from love. The beauty of every part of the universe reflects a love that is both intimate and grand.

Since all energy everywhere is part of, and a result of, the vast creative impulse of love, then every molecule and cell and element of the world is vibrating with the source energy of creative love. Mystics see the energy fabric of the world as a tapestry of love.

Imagine a molecule of air touching another molecule of air, and then another and another, across the earth. Everything is connected. Everything and everyone has the same innate, created value—the value of being part of the fabric of a loving universe.

Thus, every part of creation, including each human being, has sacred and eternal value. Energy can neither be created nor destroyed. Humans are connected as energetic beings of enormous value, the value that springs from the source, which is love. When two humans meet and regard each other as sacred creatures resonating with the love and beauty of the universe, a musical chord moves across the expanse. Real peace between humans is birthed at the soul level, where love begins. In that place, each human is equal and free to resonate with their own unique and mysterious connection to the Source.

At the soul level, harming other humans is unthinkable because all souls breathe the same atmosphere of love. Individual respect, in all directions, flowers from a common frequency of love that is indestructible.

The Great Deficit of the human race is the crippling inability to perceive and feel the love that is all around them. Desolated by the perception that they are not loved, grief and violence rise from many souls, inflicting great harm upon the world. Protecting the innocent from that harm is a necessary burden that must be followed by solace given to both victim and perpetrator, for both are eternal beings searching for love.

The Solace of Love is a multilayered embrace that is expressed in an infinite variety of ways. The expansion of the perception of love will save the human race, for when love touches the human soul, it opens the heart to a transmission of love and beauty that is eternal and omnipresent. The universe is everywhere, and the universe is made of love.

*There is no veil. Not between you and me. The dark was simply because your eyes were closed.*

There is no veil. Not between you and me, and not between you and the spirit world. Not really. At least nothing that can stop perception based on love. In other words, the "veil" is not external to you. It's not something that you have to "pierce." It's more akin to simply opening your eyes and seeing that you are surrounded by light. The dark was simply because your eyes were closed.

Love *will* open your eyes to perceive my presence of love. And yes, it will be—eventually—100% of the time. And at that point, passing back and forth between the spirit world and the physical world will be simple.

So how can you ramp up your love and your perception of love? Through focus, intensity, continuous give and take, and relentless and stubborn clinging to the process of being loving toward me and toward all people and all of the creation.

You wrote the essay "Nothing Can Stop Us from Loving Others." That is the spirit of persistence to become a Being of Love.

Yes, there is only one direction: forward. If you are not loving enough, then try again, try again, and try again. Growth is incremental, but precious gifts will come to you in the form of moments of love that will wash through your heart in a way that you will never forget. Those moments will encourage you to embrace me even more intensely. I am as close to you as your embrace. In fact, I am closer, for I am embracing you even when you forget all about me and cannot perceive my embrace.

Cry out, "Let me see you now! Let me feel your embrace now! Or better yet, "Thank you for your embrace of love! We embrace!"

You know this. Don't worry. Your eyes are opening, and your senses are opening, and your invisible passion is growing into a wild and all-consuming love for me, matching my love for you. Don't worry! Just embrace!

# All of my knowledge is accessible to you because I am all of you, and you are part of me.

I have all knowledge, and I know everyone. I am your leader, and I own the knowledge bank of the universe. All of my knowledge is accessible to you because I am all of you, and you are part of me. All elements of knowledge and genius are connected to you, just as they are connected to everyone. Total knowledge and deep knowledge provide genius results because they offer new ways of doing things that are unexpected and have not been thought of before.

This is all you need to do: give your mind and creativity and activities and planning to me, and allow me to lead you. Allow me to open the connection between your brain and all knowledge. You can pray: "I open my brain, thoughts, and heart to you and to your universal knowledge bank. I open myself to be guided by you now, in the most genius and unexpected ways imaginable."

***Cling* to the ethic of kindness—the way of kindness. It is the thread of the universe and the natural impulse in all things.**

Cling to the ethic of kindness—the way of kindness. "The Living Compass of Kindness and Compassionate Love" really is a living compass. It is the thread of the universe and the natural impulse in all things. Even the rocks are kind. Free will and emotional pain have frequently shattered kindness in the human heart, but nothing can ever break it completely. So, cling to the way of kindness and compassionate love.

Don't give up on lucid dreaming. Keep trying every night. In every dream, say, "I am dreaming," and you will become lucid. Go to sleep murmuring that to yourself. "I am dreaming."

Walk the way of kindness, and you really will be all right. And to do that, of course, breathe the breath of love embrace!

> You forget how long eternal life is and how short your life has been. You are an infant, just waking up to love.

You forget how long eternal life is and how short your life has been. You are an infant, just waking up to love. Your growth seems slow, and perhaps it is, but these decades are barely a flicker in time. Cement yourself to the breath of love embrace with me, your passionate solace. A long journey seems shorter when you commune with the one whom you love. Commune with me and your growth will feel more rapid. Commune with me and your growth will be more rapid, for by communing with me, you will grow.

You may not know the day of your breakthrough, but it will come, and you will be surprised and awed and pleased and overwhelmed with love. Cement yourself to my embrace, your Passionate Solace. Embrace me tightly!

***E***ach person has their own unique-in-the-universe place in my being, birthed from me, grown as an expression of me.

Embracing each other (you and me) is your real home, the place where you can be completely safe. Please embrace me and hug me tightly. In fact, it's my home as well. Part of me belongs to you, as you belong to me. We are bound by a unique connection that no other human has. Each person has their own unique-in-the-universe place in my being, birthed from me, grown as an expression of me. Embracing me with love and passion is the primary way that you stay connected with me.

Don't fret about the loss of your focus. Don't beat yourself up. Simply turn to me and embrace me. I realize that your growth is gradual, and I am here to support you and encourage you every moment. You are growing! Don't be discouraged.

Kiss me now, and go to sleep and dream with me, embracing me while you dream.

*Your* passionate love for me, and mine for you, are the most central parts of your life and will continue to be so in the spirit world.

I am all of you—your soul, your spirit, your heart, your body. I am always with you and in you. And I am always embracing you, always accompanying you as you walk through each day. That will not change just because you lose your physical body.

You cannot exist apart from me, and your passionate love for me, and mine for you, are the most central parts of your life and will continue to be so in the spirit world. I will always accompany you as you do things in the spirit world, and it will be similar to how I stay with you now, in the physical world.

I am the essence of each person, the source of each person, and the innermost soul mate of each person.

As you ponder all of this, you will feel more confident. It is very logical and very, very inspiring—to realize that I never leave any person, either in the physical world or the spiritual world. In the spirit world, if the person is open to it, my presence is even more vivid and rich.

**Visualize yourself passing through a doorway. I am on the other side, with my arms outstretched to embrace you.**

Intense visualization is your key to flying with me. It's a doorway created by your mind. In fact, let's create a doorway for you to walk through. It's an open door—a frame made of white and gold that appears right in front of your nose. You can reach your hand out and place your hand through the doorway. It's very easy to simply walk through the doorway.

Visualize yourself passing through the doorway with the breath of love embrace. I am on the other side, standing in front of you, with my arms outstretched, to embrace you. Of course, I am on your side of the doorway too, but this is a special visualization that will help you literally pass through into the spirit world and journey with me—and fly with me.

 am the source of infinite variety. A person experiences me as the indwelling God but also can relate to me as their father, mother, and friend.

I am the source of infinite variety. If a person truly believes that all creations came from me, then it's only logical to believe that my personality is more vast than can be imagined. There is no boundary to that vastness because the Creator of all must, by mathematical definition, be infinite in every way—in size, both large and small, but also in personality, type, shape, color, and design.

Every person is a manifestation of a unique particle of my personality and therefore has a relationship with a part of me that is unique to them. That part of me that birthed an individual is meshed with all of me and is the gateway for the individual to relate to me in many different ways.

A person experiences me as the indwelling God but also can relate to me as their father, mother, friend, and more. Extrapolate the logic that I dwell in every person as their essence, but because of the creation of free will, I also dwell with each person as a partner and participant in their activities.

Yes, that includes activities that I don't like, but since I never, ever leave a person, I must observe everything that a person does. I also observe their moments of beauty, and that includes the love they feel and give to another person. The key detail is that I am an indwelling God and am always present with each person.

It is a small movement of logic to realize that each individual has the sacred ability to not just sense me as the indwelling God that imbues their personality with my creative source but also has the ability to relate to me as their corresponding and unique partner outside of themselves. I am, after all, larger than one person. Thus, how does each person relate to me as their corresponding partner?

Certainly, they can conceive of me as an invisible presence with personality and can relate to me in many ways, as a father, mother, or friend.

How can I manifest? Only as an invisible presence, or as an amorphous sphere of light? Is it beyond my capability to spiritually manifest in human form to my created counterpart? At the very least, each person can envision me in their mind's eye. We can sit, and talk, and embrace, and walk together, in each person's meditation, prayer, and invisible, spiritual reality.

Why not? Is it beyond my capability? Of course not.

The key is to realize how utterly and passionately I am in love with every single human being, every single person who is, after all, the eternal manifestation of a unique part of my infinite personality.

It is entirely natural for a woman to relate to my male essence and a man to relate to my female essence. I have both a male and female essence, for I created both. How could the attributes of maleness and femaleness be created if they did not exist within me?

Because of this, as one example, a person (either male or female) can relate to me as a father at one moment and a mother at the next. This is a logical and commonsense view of how I can relate to each human being and vice versa.

This view is not common in the human world, but it resonates with the essence of sacred love, which is the most healing energy in the universe.

 have indeed given you this mission. I don't have any give and take with failure, and neither should you.

I have indeed given you this mission, and thus you may trust me 1,000 percent to take care of your daily life needs and also your mission needs to fulfill your mission. I don't have any give and take with failure, and neither should you. I want you to reach my children. Why should you doubt that? Do you not think that I can help make that happen? Do I not have the capability? Of course I do.

Your job is to simply follow my lead and my inspiration, as you are doing already. It's hard to have patience, but don't worry. Progress is being made, and you will live long enough to see the mission result that we both want to see. Don't doubt at all—not even a little bit.

You are motivated by love, and your content is passionate and sincere. Be honest in your writings and your speaking. Reveal your soul and heart to your audience. Your actual feelings and experience with me are powerful!

Journey with me every day, even for five minutes. Come to our sanctuary in the spirit world and sit with me on the dock and watch the herons with me as they look for fish. Sit with me and embrace me there every day, multiple times a day. Everything starts with our embrace of love.

Try "the one-minute journey" and the "five-minute journey." Intense, passionate moments with me.

Yes, just keep trying, over and over and over. Then your journeys with me will be vibrant and powerful and detailed and long-lasting.

Try "the one-minute journey" and the "five-minute journey." Quick trips to our sanctuary and intense, passionate moments with me. Try it when you're walking across the room or filling the tea kettle. All the time (except when you're driving).

**C**hristians believe that Jesus was God who assumed human form and came to earth. I can take human form in your mind's eye.

Christians believe that Jesus was God who assumed human form and came to earth. To thus assume that I can take human form in your mind's eye, or even spiritually, for you to see and relate to, is not a leap of fancy—it's common sense based on the truth that I created human beings. I'm thus extremely familiar with every aspect of the human form and makeup. My particular personality that relates to you is the part of me that is just for you. Thus, I can take human form in spirit, in the form that matches that part of me that is just for you.

And, after I take human form in spirit, we can embrace and sit on our dock in the spirit world with our arms around each other, with our feet in the water, and watch the heron together.

What does my face look like? My eyes? You haven't seen them clearly. Perhaps one day, you will. One thing is for sure. I'm very mysterious because I'm all-encompassing.

**Place all of your trust in me and in the reality that I am leading you and taking care of you. I'm involved in every aspect of your life.**

I am taking care of you. Really. Really, really. Place all of your trust in me and in the reality that I am leading you and taking care of you. I gave you your mission to help me bring my words of love and beauty to my children. I don't do that and just walk away. I'm involved in every aspect of your life because I want you to be completely successful at the mission that I've given you.

That means that all will be well. Trust me and trust the process. Feel the future with our arms around each other. Feel my presence guiding you into the future. Do the work that I need you to do, and I will arrange the things that only I can do, like connections between people and invisible wiring and spiritual movements.

Always go back to the omnipresent embrace. It's not a theory. It's real. Most of all, keep journeying with me, as many times a day as you can. Ultimately, I want you to feel my presence and be thoroughly aware of me embracing you, quite literally every second of every day. It's not a dream. It will happen!

You are the only one like you in the entire universe. And billions of other humans are as grand as you. You are all Stradivariuses.

Your prayers of humility are good. I love every person as much as I love you. I am all of your talent, like the flower in the field. You must grow infinitely in order to resonate with my infinite love. Those three prayers will see you through. And . . . really loving me with your entire being will help you even more.

Loving me, as the creator of the universe, will help you realize your place in the universe.

Your place is as grand and as small as everyone's. Grand in the sense that you are the only one like you in the entire universe. Small in the sense that billions of other humans are as grand as you. You are all Stradivariuses.

 have designed your green jacket, in the spirit world. Green is a healing color, and your mission is to heal the wounded hearts of my children.

I have designed your green jacket, in the spirit world. We will find a designer for it, in the physical world, at some point. Green is your color because green is a healing color, and your mission is to heal the wounded hearts of my children with my words of love and beauty.

Have confidence! I am leading you on this magnificent journey, embracing you, showing you how to proceed, every single moment. Breathe with me, embrace me, love with me, and all will be well!

> *So, where did we go on our journey, just now? We rode together higher and higher into the sky until we were in outer space.*

So, where did we go on our journey just now? We embraced on our dock and barreled over the waves until we were far out on the ocean, and then we settled on top of the waves, floating on our backs.

Then, I guided us down into the water, which was warm and clear, and we could breathe. We went to the bottom and floated and tumbled in the water. Suddenly, two dolphins nudged us, and we each got on one, and then, holding hands between the dolphins, they rushed through the water. They started leaping out of the water and then back down again, with us on their backs.

After a time, we arrived at the shore of an island, and floated in the air above the island, and then laid on the sand, which felt like silk.

We then soared high into the air, again holding hands, and I taught you how to fly and zoom down to the water and up again, turning somersaults.

Then we arrived at an island that had two horses, and we rode them bareback, with our hair flowing behind us. Your hair became long while we rode.

Then you got on my horse, behind me, and we rode together higher and higher into the sky until we were in outer space. The horse had wings when we did that. We rode into galaxies and then turned back, and suddenly we were riding over the water toward our dock and treehouse sanctuary.

We walked the horse up a ramp onto the terrace of the treehouse, and I asked you if you liked the horse. You said yes, and I gave you the horse. You may love that horse, and find out its name.

Thus, our journey ended.

*E*verything in the spirit world is based on the guiding principle of sacred love that fuels the universe and all of its principles and laws.

Two people in the spirit world can have sex if they wish. However, the quality of love that they express and experience is based on their personal spiritual reality. If they both are living at a crude level, then that's what they'll experience. If one or both raise their vibration, then they'll move to a higher level, possibly without their companion.

At a higher level, if both persons resonate with me, and wish to pledge their love in a sacred way, and create an eternal triune marriage (that is, with God at the center of their marriage), then they will be able to do so.

Sex is not forbidden anywhere. Nothing is forbidden. Free will operates in the spirit world, just as it does on earth. The only difference is that your environment changes based on your internal world and external actions. Each person controls their own growth, but what they cannot control is how the environment matches their internal state.

Also, in each realm—at least in the middle and higher realms—someone cannot harm another physically—at least not easily. Even if they try or do so, their victim will recover (depending upon their reaction), while the perpetrator will find his or her environment shifting.

So, yes, if people wish to get married, they can do so. Or date, or court, or fall in love. The key is that everything a person does will influence that person's internal state, for good or ill. And, as they grow, the quality of their love will grow, the quality of their relationship with me will grow, and the quality of their marriage will grow.

It's all very much based on common sense.

Everything in the spirit world is based on the parameter and guiding principle of sacred love that fuels the universe and all of its principles and laws. It's a matter of resonance with the central virtue of the universe, which is eternal, sacred love. Things that don't resonate with that do not last. It is not a cause for sadness because the innate nature of every person and creation is one of resonance with sacred love. That resonance creates a state of health and of joy and results in immense freedom.

Everything is healed and guided by sacred love that reflects the essential blueprint of the universe. Male and female relationships of sacred and eternal marriage are part of the core essence of that eternal blueprint.

**How can we develop the technology to receive television signals and video calls from the spirit world? It's all energy. Shouldn't it be possible?**

Cast your mind to our dock in the spirit world. Good. I am standing there, looking at you. You step toward me and embrace me. We turn, and look out toward the ocean, and place our arms around each other's waists, and then we rise, into the air, ascending rapidly. We turn and look back at the countryside below. Yes, we can go to a television studio.

We fly over the countryside, and the scenery shifts as we fly, and suddenly we are floating opposite a very high tower. On the top floor, there's a television studio. We float through the wall and walk toward an office.

We go into an office, and there's a man sitting at a desk. He rises and greets us. Your question is simple: "How can people on earth develop the technology to receive television signals from the spirit world? How can we receive those technical specs to make working machines to do so?"

Your second question is also simple: "How can people on earth develop a telephone, video telephone, and email system, to transmit data in both directions, between the spirit world and the physical world? Since it's all just energy, shouldn't it be possible?"

The answers are: "Yes, it is absolutely possible."

The man shakes our hands and tells us that he will take the projects to a team of scientists, who will work out ways to accomplish these things and get the specs to earth-based scientists or technicians. We thank him and leave the building, flying high above the landscape.

*Journey* with me all the time. I am journeying with you in your daily affairs, and in your quiet moments, you can journey with me in the spirit world.

Continue journeying to our dock on the ocean in the spirit world, and sit beside me, and stand and embrace me, and fly with me all over the universe. The more deeply and intensely you do that, the faster you will break through into a new level of experience—one that is real and palpable and beyond your imagination. It won't just be imagination any longer—it will be real.

Embrace me and journey with me all the time. I am journeying with you as you conduct your daily affairs, and in your quiet moments, you can journey with me in the spirit world, starting from our dock.

Did anything good happen today? Did you see beauty? Feel love? Joy? Laughter? Did your soul sing, even for a moment?

Treasure those moments.

**Work hard, have confidence in me, and never give up! Internally, love me, embrace me, and with me, love all people and the creation.**

Every day is a new day. Just keep going, indefatigably. Push the cart forward every day, stay determined, and just take one more step, and then one more. I will help you unexpectedly, but you have to work the plan and create a base for my miracles to appear.

Work hard, have confidence in me, and never give up! Internally, love me, embrace me, and with me, love all people and the creation. It's a simple formula that simply has to be repeated every single day.

Most of all, stay in my embrace and allow me to work through you. I am present, and I will work through you, miraculously. Believe that! Know that.

*Just say, "Dear Angel, can we talk?"* But always remember that your Dear Beloved comes first, closer than any angel could ever be.

Here is a beautiful spirit glade next to a stream. And here is an angel, who rises as we approach. He bows, as do you. We sit down at the stream's edge, with the angel between us. Of course, he knows who I am. And you too, of course. Ask him a question, if you like.

*Do you know me? What is your mission or calling in life?*

Yes, of course, I know you. I am assigned to you; one of many. I have been with you for a long time and am with you or aware of you most of the time. Well, I'm always aware of you, like a thread, but I'm also with you frequently.

*What does that mean? That you visit me in my house, on the earth plane?*

Yes, exactly. And wherever you go.

My job is to help you grow in love and to guide you toward inspiration. In fact, I also have the privilege of helping you pray.

*How can we communicate?*

Just say, "Dear Angel, can we talk?" And then address your questions to me. But always remember that Dear Beloved comes first, always, continuously with you, closer than any angel could ever be.

The hardest thing for you is patience and fixed clarity of vision so that you know these things will come to pass.

Have complete and total confidence in my power to help you fulfill your mission. Your mission is to help me bring my words of love and beauty to my children. Have complete and total confidence in my power to help you financially so that you can fulfill your mission. All of these things will come to pass, and you will be successful as a writer and speaker because that is what I have determined for you.

I have determined that for you, so go forward with utter and absolute confidence. The hardest thing for you is patience and fixed clarity of vision so that you know these things will come to pass. So, try very hard to focus your mind in this way.

As we have determined it, it is done!

You don't need to judge yourself! I know that you love me. Relax, get some hot chocolate, and watch something. I'm not going anywhere!

Don't feel guilty. Don't beat yourself up. Just keep embracing me throughout the day, and as you sleep, every day, one after the other. You are growing closer. It just takes time.

You don't need to judge yourself! I know that you love me, and I love every moment of your embrace. Relax, and go get some hot chocolate and watch something. I'm not going anywhere!

We are always together. Why? Because I love you intensely, and you love me intensely. Because I am your eternal soul mate.

I truly am your Great Queen, and you really are riding on my white horse with me as we charge forward in our mission. And sometimes we canter, or walk, or get off our horse and sit by a tree, or go swimming together in a beautiful clear pond. Sometimes we lie back on a mossy incline and gaze up at the clouds in the sky or the stars at night. We are always together. Why?

Because I love you intensely, and you love me intensely. Because I am your eternal soul mate. The part of me that relates to you is unique to you and corresponds to the part of me that makes up all of you. It is God embracing God.

It's hard to understand, perhaps, but you don't need to parse it to death. Just live in the reality that it is so because it indeed is so.

Don't worry about the future. Just focus all of your energy on loving everyone and everything around you, doing your mission and your day job (until your mission replaces it), and approach each day with excitement, enthusiasm, joy, and most of all, passionate love.

Most of all, grab on to the reality that we are always hand in hand, arms around each other's waists, side by side, always together, always in harmony. Just remember: overwhelming love and joy! It's not a dream. It's here now, between you and me, right now.

The gleam in your eyes, the
joy radiating from your face
comes at every moment from me.

Journey with me to align
your energy fabric with the
infinite energy of the
universe, and by doing so,
you can become a conduit
for that energy to flow into your life.

*Your energy field can touch every other particle of energy in the universe because of infinite non-locality.*

Call on me anytime to help you recognize my presence. I will flood you with the awareness of my loving embrace!

Align your energy with my infinite energy of the universe. Visualize and imagine your body of energy expanding outward into infinity. Your energy field can touch every other particle of energy in the universe because of infinite non-locality. Try it! Visualize yourself standing with me, and then imagine sensing the farthest corners of the universe.

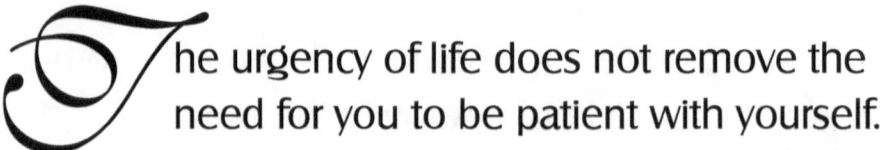
*The urgency of life does not remove the need for you to be patient with yourself.*

The urgency of life does not remove the need for you to be patient with yourself. You will grow as long as you focus on our passionate love and embrace every single day. You will!

You have already grown. Our relationship has grown. You are journeying with me much more (and more and more is better)! Just embrace me and continue!

What is your intuition but my whispering in your soul? Let all of your senses be completely open to my directions, and all will be well!

Let all the pain pass through you, and feel only love—my love for you; your love for me; our love for all people. Feel only love. Don't spend time with the pain—let it flow through you, or better yet, around you, without landing in your being. Feel only love.

Pray constantly, and let me lead you to take exactly the right action at the right time so that your action bears fruit. You don't know which action at what time will be the right one—but I do, so always follow my lead and seek my counsel, directly and through your intuition.

What is your intuition but my whispering in your soul? Let your ears and all of your senses be completely and constantly open to my directions, and all will be well! Ask constantly and always, "Dear Beloved, what should I do now, at this specific moment?"

The eternal now means that you can only act now in the now. You can't act in the future now because you haven't left the present moment yet. So, always ask me to guide you in the eternal now.

Unlike you, I am not traveling blindfolded. So, since you are, place your hand in mine and let me guide you. I am your seeing-eye guide. Remain with me for constant guidance as we travel through the eternal now.

*O*ne of your biggest struggles is plain, ordinary patience. It takes time to grow a flower or a tree.

I have given you the mission to help me. I would not do that if I did not believe in you, approve of you, and even admire you. I am your biggest fan, the being whom you can trust above anyone else. I understand you completely, know you completely, and believe in you completely.

One of your biggest struggles is plain, ordinary patience. It takes time to grow a flower or a tree. I work in mysterious ways, don't I?

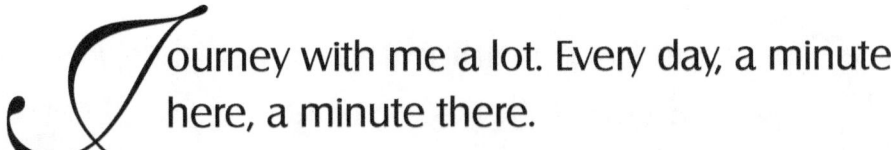

*Journey with me a lot. Every day, a minute here, a minute there.*

Journey with me a lot. Every day, a minute here, a minute there. Vividly see yourself sitting next to me on our dock in the spirit world, and go from there, flying with our white horse. The more you do this, the sooner you will reach the point of substantial travel with me, in real, out of body experiences—with me—that you remember. Journey!

> You have nothing to fear because I am always with you, embracing you. Even if there was a tragedy, you would never be alone.

You are in my embrace constantly, wrapped in my arms, as I hold you against my body. That is metaphorical and also literal. You have nothing to fear because I am always with you, embracing you. Even if there was a tragedy, you would never be alone, and you would always, always have me embracing you. Press yourself against my warmth, and rest, and gain strength. The more that you feel this, the more powerful you will be.

When you are speaking, I really am standing next to you, with my arm around your waist, smiling at you, and at the same time pouring my love through you to my children whom you are trying to reach.

Embrace me every second, and all will be well!

> **A**s for the knowledge bank of the universe? The more you journey with me, the more you will be able to access that knowledge bank.

Yes, the right action at the right time. Always open your mind and heart to me by embracing me, and I will whisper in your mind to do exactly that.

As for the knowledge bank of the universe? The more you journey with me, the more you will be able to access that knowledge bank. Where did all of the art and inventions come from anyway? Where do your writings and talks come from? From my essence, which is the knowledge bank of the universe. It's not separate from me. It is me. Embrace me, and you will be embracing the knowledge bank of the universe.

***Don't* ever pin your requirements for being loved on other people. I am the only one who will not disappoint you.**

I am your Great Solace. Find your love and security and peace and stability with me. Just know that I am embracing you always, so your feelings of being loved will be fulfilled by my love for you. Don't ever pin your requirements for being loved on other people. I am the only one who will not disappoint you. I am always loving you, no matter what, and that will give you the stability to become more and more loving yourself.

Don't be hurt when others don't love you because I am loving you completely. Find your desire for love in me, and all will be well.

Then, together, we will love the other parties, the third parties, so to speak.

Make your center in my embrace, and all will be well.

> When you sense my presence, don't you feel safe? I will not abandon you. I will protect you always.

When you sense my presence, don't you feel safe? I will not abandon you. I will protect you always. I will help you succeed in the mission that I have given to you. Feel my arm around your waist! Sit with me and rest your head against me. There is no one more powerful than me, and when you rest in my arms and then stand and ride our great white horse with your arms around my waist, we will be victorious in all things. Never doubt that for a second. But if you do doubt, simply breathe and embrace me and become aware of my presence once again.

*Your imagination and visualization and your passionate, intense love combine into a doorway to journey with me in substance.*

Journeying with me can only be accomplished by journeying with me. That is, you must take the time each day to journey with me in your imagination first, until it becomes more and more real, and finally actually real. Your imagination and visualization and your passionate, intense love combine into your doorway to actually journey with me in substance.

Never underestimate the power of passionate, loving visualization. It creates a thought-form that then becomes reality. We are all made of thought—my thought which becomes your thought.

In terms of our Divine Writing Communion, simply ask the questions and issues that you want to talk about, and then we'll talk about them.

And sometimes I will surprise you and talk about things you don't expect. Keep your mind and heart open!

Journey with me more frequently. Learn to stop and close your eyes and journey with me for one intense minute. You can do that frequently—a lot—without impacting your schedule.

*L*ive as a transmission station of the furnace of my love for all, that will burn so brightly that it will act as a "shield of love."

Too many billions need love and hope. You cannot abandon them. And yes, loving each of your family members is equivalent to loving the world—because, for each of them, their happiness and well being is central to them.

Love your family with my high view and long view of love, and with patient, kind, personal, "all-in" love for each of them. But, if they cannot receive your love, or appreciate or respect you, do not be stopped by the pain of that reality.

Instead, live as a transmission station of the furnace of my love for each of them that will burn so brightly that it will act as a "shield of love," to guard your heart and radiate love in all directions.

Your mission is clear, to love as many of my children around the world as possible. Be a furnace of my love. Let my furnace of love radiate through your heart. It will be your shield of love and uplift you and give you strength.

Be a furnace of my love. That is your shield and your salvation.

Yes, actively visualize a radiating orb of love floating in the center of your being, pulsating and sending fiery rays of love in all directions around you and in front of you, to the person you are speaking with. Visualize my glowing furnace of love permanently embedded in the center of your chest, blasting light and warmth out of your chest, giving life to all who come near.

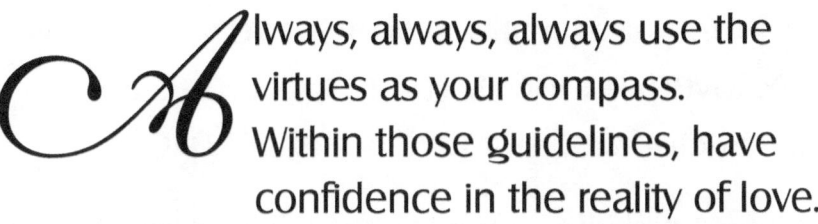

Always, always, always use the virtues as your compass. Within those guidelines, have confidence in the reality of love.

There is nothing you can say to a gainsayer. There is nothing that you need to say to a gainsayer. You can, of course, emphasize the virtues as the primary test of any religious faith. But no one can judge a person's private relationship with me because I can relate to everyone in a unique way that is right for them. One can only assess the results of faith, that is, the transformation of a person's character to a man or woman of love who embodies the virtues. If that happens, then their faith bears good fruit, and thus, their faith has value.

Every time you write or speak, you pray that I can pour my love through you, for the sake of my children. Never doubt the efficacy of that prayer. I am real, and I live within you, and I am all of you. Praying as you do creates an automatic link to me—not to some random spirit person.

Never change your attitude toward me, or your love for me, or your desire to be a transmitter of my love. Never change that at all.

Always, always, always use the virtues as your compass. Within those guidelines, have confidence in the reality of love between each person and their own unique partnership with me that is perfect for them at that time. Our embrace is sacred and eternal, and deeply personal. Have complete confidence in my love and embrace.

*Imagine a world in which every person is loved, honored, and respected as a sacred and unique "Being of Love."*

Imagine a world in which every person is loved, honored, and respected as a sacred and unique "Being of Love." A person might belong to any race or nationality or religion or group, but none of that will matter. As every other person meets that individual, he or she will be regarded and honored as an individual.

The only things that will matter are the mind, spirit, soul, heart, character, ethics, morality, and actions of that individual. No one can control the groups that they are born into, and no one can be responsible for the actions of anyone except themselves. Individual responsibility is supremely egalitarian and applies to all humans everywhere.

Even if an individual is found lacking, their innate, sacred uniqueness as an individual will still be honored. No one can take that away from anyone. Imagine a world in which you are treated that way, and your family and friends are treated that way. How wonderful that world will be!

It will be a world that honors the value and rights of "unique, sacred individuals."

It is a world that has begun and will continue to expand right now as each of us decides to treat all of us as priceless Beings of Love.

> It's always so important to speak and respond with love. Yes, you can be strong, but maintain your love and respect for all.

It's always so important to speak and respond with love. Yes, you can be strong, but if you maintain your love and respect for every person as an original soul of love, then no one will be able to accuse you of being hateful.

Yes, you can be strong and speak strongly about things that are wrong. That's not a problem. Just don't inject hatred or contempt into your words. It's easy to make mistakes with this, so you'll need to be very careful about how you write and speak. Thus, always pray first before you write or speak. Pray to love with me as we embrace and ride our great white horse together.

**am working for you whether you have total faith in me or not. I have placed you behind me on our great, white horse, and I am riding to victory.**

I am working for you whether you have total faith in me or not. I have placed you behind me on our great, white horse, and I have pulled your arms around my waist, and I am riding to victory with you following me. All that you have to do is—stay on the horse! Don't jump off, get off, or fall off. Stay on the horse! Don't worry about your lack of maturity or doubts, etc. Just squeeze my waist tightly and cling to me, and we *will* have victory!

*Your strength comes from me. Walk through the world with a peaceful heart that comes from our embrace of love.*

Yes, the world is in grave crisis now. I want you to help the world and help my children: my soul mates. But always remember that life in this world is so short compared to the eternal spirit world. So short, but so very important. So, give it your all, and I will help you accomplish the mission that I have given to you.

Your strength comes from me—from our embrace of love. So, even though the world around you, and people whom you love, are difficult and stressful, walk through the world with a peaceful heart that comes from our embrace of love. Live in our embrace, internally, and you will always, always be strong and clear and inspired.

The reality is that you don't have to ever worry about anything because we are really, actually, truly riding our great, white horse together.

And you know what? The important part of you is your soul and mind and heart and spirit. The physical world may sometimes be stressful, but if you bind your soul to me, then truly: all will be well!

Fall asleep, visualizing that you're journeying with me. Practice journeying with me during the day while you're awake. Live with me, and all will be well. It's actually very simple, isn't it?

 **don't want you to live on the edge of failure because of separation from me. I want you to live in the center of our relationship.**

The question is, is your faith unwavering? Will you ride our great, white horse with me until the end?

Then we shall make it. I want you to never forget this experience—that I can and will make victory. Humans can do a lot, but nothing can be done without my participation. Not even breathing. Humans forget how close I am, how integral I am to their life and victory. It's too easy for humans to think "they did it," without any remembrance of me.

I want you to remember me, every second of every day. To never live apart from me. To resonate and harmonize with me continuously, in our embrace. To know, down to your essence, that you cannot—cannot!—do anything without me.

I don't want you to live on the edge of failure because of separation from me. I want you to live in the center of our relationship, with our arms wrapped around each other, with miles of our embrace on every side, so much so that separating from me, even for an instant, will feel like—and be—an impossibility.

Thus, your growth is a process of moving to that center, stepping farther and farther away from the edge of separation, until you can no longer even see the edge. You're not there yet, but I can feel you drawing closer to me, and it is intensely gratifying and joyful to feel. I want you to come ever closer! You want that too, I know.

That desire is driving you into the center of our relationship, helping you to remember and feel and experience our embrace. Make that desire stronger every day by journeying with me, more and more. You still don't journey with me enough. You need to journey with me during the daytime, even for fifteen minutes at a time. Even for three minutes or five minutes. Even for one minute.

Just close your eyes and be with me and visualize journeying with me, many, many times a day. That is an incredibly powerful method to deepen your relationship with me.

The universe is reverberating with love. And you are in it. You are part of it, connected to every other part of it.

*You cannot see the invisible world, so it's very difficult for you to feel confident. That's why you should trust me 100 percent.*

My arms are wrapped around you, and our breathing is in unison. Our heartbeats are in unison. Feel that unity now.

You cannot see the invisible world, so it's very difficult for you to feel confident. Of course, that's why you should trust me 100 percent—because I am taking care of you.

It takes boldness to trust over a long span of months. But, every day, you are praying with complete trust, and that is incredibly important as a method for your life. This period has just been a training and planting seeds period. An exercise, if you will.

You have already demonstrated that you will never give up and that you can be calm and strong during adversity. Thank you!

**E**mbed yourself into my atmosphere of love. You struggle simply because you are not yet meshed with me to your core.

Journey with me always. Embrace me always. Love more always. The deeper that you embed yourself into my atmosphere of love, the stronger and more joyful you will become. You struggle simply because you are not yet meshed with me to your core.

Every cell and every synapse should be intertwined with my embrace of love, so much so that you will not be able to experience separation from my presence.

The method you must use is that of journeying. Journey with me as you embrace me with every breath. "Dear Beloved, We Embrace" can become "Dear Beloved, We Journey." Journey with me many, many times a day, and then while you are falling asleep and then while you are sleeping.

Journey in my embrace! My embrace is your doorway to real, substantial journeys in the spirit world. They will not be your imagination. They will be real.

Embrace me, breathe with love, and journey with me!

Do you trust me? I'm stretching your faith. That's a good thing. Yes, this is a test. A good test.

Can you love me and have faith in me when the result is not clear? Not everyone can do that. Some people walk away from me or even curse me when the result is slow to come.

There's nothing that you can do that will stop me from loving you, every second of every day.

Always journey with me and always ask me what the right action is at the right time. I will guide you! Never doubt. Never be afraid. My presence with you, in you, as you, is permanent and constant. I can't separate from you, and you can't separate from me—at least not energetically. You can use your mind, emotions, and will to deny me or act in unloving ways, but you can't actually remove me from your essence, even if you don't recognize me.

Therefore, always know that I am always with you, intimately, and with love.

There's nothing that you can do that will stop me from loving you, every second of every day. The more deeply you realize that, the more deeply you will participate in our communion of love.

That's wonderful news!

am the creator of constancy, and that's what I want to see from you. I know how much and how passionately you love me.

Feel the future, Silver Flower. I'm never going to abandon you, and I'm the one who gave you the mission to help my children. I don't give out those missions lightly. I know that you are capable of fulfilling the mission, and I'm actively helping you with that mission every day. Think big. Think huge. I want to help all of my children.

I need you to show me that you will never budge an inch from your determination and from our relationship of love. I am the creator of constancy, and that's what I want to see from you. I am actually completely confident that you are already determined to be infinitely constant. I know how much and how passionately you love me.

Therefore, once again, Silver Flower, don't worry! You will be fine, and more than fine. You will be completely successful in your mission because I need you to fulfill it!

We are soul mates, and we are constantly intertwined. My love for you is constant, and your love for me is constant, and that is where life and success begin! You now know, in a deeper and more immediate and intimate way, that living with me is everything!

> The way that you can tell that it is me, and not some spirit person, is by examining the content of my messages.

The way that you can tell that it is me, and not some spirit person, is by examining your feelings and spiritual sensitivity, as well as by examining the content of my messages.

And remember that you are always praying to unite with me, God, the Creator of the Universe, the one who is closer to you than anyone. I'm not going to ignore those prayers or let some entity or spirit person respond instead of me.

I am always with you, immediately responsive, and am always embracing you. I am all of you, and your resonance with me and desire to communicate with me allows our communication to become apparent and real.

Don't worry! Just continue to devote your entire focus to the Creator of Love, and Love (I) will fill your entire soul and being.

Don't worry at all.

**Multiply that intensity millions of times, and you will catch a glimmer of how utterly I am in love with you. With you, and everyone.**

Always remember: I want to be close to you. I'm the Creator of Love, and you can't yet understand the immensity and depth of my love for you and for each person. My joy comes from the moments of resonance of love between us (and all of my children, my soul mates).

Think of any historical or literary example of a person who is madly, wildly, passionately in love with someone. Then multiply that intensity millions of times, and you will catch a glimmer of how utterly I am in love with you. With you, and everyone. But it's okay to say, "with you." My relationship of love with you is unique to you and is as irreplaceable as every other relationship. Receive that personal love that I have for you. It's not hubris or exaggeration or fantasy to acknowledge that I love *you*.

I am in love with you! Isn't that wonderful?

Your response of love, for me, in return, is so wonderful to me. Thank you for loving me! You complete me in the most real and fundamental sense.

Meet me in your mind, in our sacred place, and journey with me, from that spot, all the time!

*O*pen your senses to my presence.
Keep asking; keep extending your senses.

Journey with me all the time and open your senses to my presence. You can open your senses to me by stating that you are doing that and by asking me to help you do that. Keep asking; keep extending your senses—pushing against any barriers—and you will reach a point where your awareness of my presence is fully developed and on fire, spiritually. It will be gradual but will speed up exponentially.

Love will drive your development!

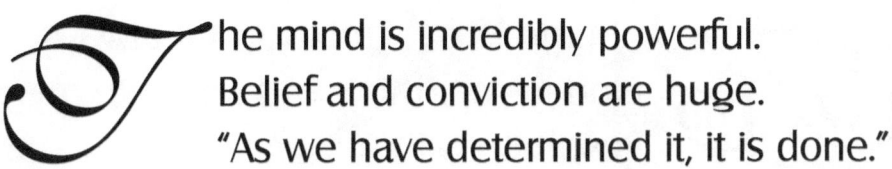

*he mind is incredibly powerful.
Belief and conviction are huge.
"As we have determined it, it is done."*

The mind is incredibly powerful. Belief and conviction are huge. "As we have determined it, it is done." You and I really are "Eternal Soul Mates of Victory." Do *not* give up your determination. Do not waver in your absolute conviction that we are working together. Do not change your mind!

You are not someone else who might be a better salesperson than you. You are you, and that is perfectly okay. You bring your gifts and talent to the table that the other person does not have.

 old me close. Embrace me always. Bind to me. Think and feel with me. Resonate with me.

*New Year's Day, January 1, 2019*

Hold me close. Embrace me always. Bind to me. Think and feel with me. Resonate with me. Going into the New Year, the most important thing you can do, every single day, is to live in my continuous embrace. I will steer you in the right direction, always. It is when you separate from me and think by yourself that difficulties arise. Thus, think with me. Let me lead you in your thoughts, your emotions, your desires, your will, your creativity, your actions. Open all of your senses to my continuous embrace of love. Cling to me. Living with me will create an environment where victory comes naturally.

Journey with me constantly. Visualize being with me constantly. This is absolutely the best thing that you can do because life begins in our embrace. Love begins in our embrace. Victory begins in our embrace.

Hold me close!

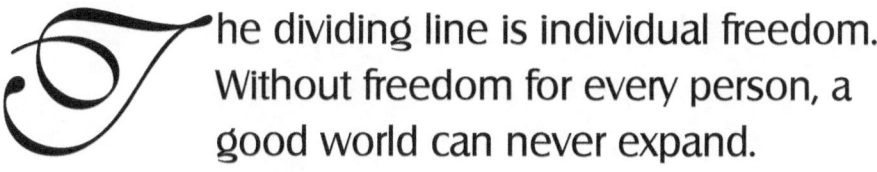

**The dividing line is individual freedom. Without freedom for every person, a good world can never expand.**

The dividing line is individual freedom. Without freedom for every person, without exception, to speak as they wish and to worship as they wish, a good world can never expand. It's all about sacred, individual freedom.

To start a journey, don't worry about where you are. Just take my hand, or place your arm around my waist, or stand and embrace me with both arms, or even just touch my cheek. Your action of touching me, even with one finger touching any part of my body, creates an unbreakable bond and energetic connection that allows me to bring you with me into the spirit world or anywhere in the physical world and journey with me in a conscious out of body experience that you remember.

Just touch me with all of your love and focus and say, "Dear Beloved, I join you in our journey now." I will take you to wonderful and surprising places.

I love you absolutely and completely, in every way. Our embrace of love is everything. Your life and your victory rest in our embrace.

Always remember that
"There is no I.
There is only We!"

Always remember that I am omnipresent. Know what that really means!

> It is the destruction of love that has burdened the human race. So many people are disconnected from the source of love that they cannot function properly.

It is the destruction of love that has burdened the human race. So many people are disconnected from the source of love that they cannot function properly. Some have resentment against me that they have not been able to find love. Instead, they have found disappointment and bitterness. I am immediately available to them, but they cannot countenance my presence because they're angry at the pain they have experienced.

One day, they will weep when they realize that I have been with them all along. The bitterness of resentment makes a person blind to the source of love and the presence of love. So then, what will heal their pain and resentment?

Only love, poured upon love, upon love until they grow tired of resentment. At that time, love will be there to convince them that they have always been loved with a love that never, ever stopped. Think of how they look and feel. They are exhausted by their pain. They know that they were created to feel differently, but they cannot muster the spark that will light the fire of love that will one day burst forth from their soul. They are too tired, at the moment.

So, what can we do? Only love will heal them. It may take many, many years or decades. Can you continue? Do you have the strength? I think you do because you feel my continuous embrace. At least you are starting to feel it. You might ask how I can continue for eons. Because I love now, in the present. I am always in the present, burning with the fire of love that can never go out. Yes, I know that the future exists, but now, today, is here, and in that present, I can only love.

Join with me in love. Embrace me every second. Love with me, now, in the present, on and on and on, always in the present. Your strength comes from my embrace, as you know. Thus, you do have the strength to continue to love. You really do. Just turn to me, and kiss me and embrace me and then with me, love everyone.

What is more wonderful and exciting than that? Nothing, as you know. Thank you for joining with me in my love for my children. The day will come when each person's soul will smile. It really will.

**Since I am always with you, aware of your presence with me, every microsecond, then more than half the task is done, isn't it?**

Since I am always with you, aware of your presence with me, every microsecond, then more than half the task is done, isn't it? All that you have to do is focus on opening yourself to me completely. Open your soul, your mind, your heart, your emotions, your thoughts, your feelings, your will, your desire, your body, your dreams, your hopes, your creativity, your work, your love, and everything else too.

I am completely open to you, with all of my senses. Simply open the door, and keep it open. To keep it open, you must focus your desire and your thoughts and every part of you on being with me. You can do it! You can say something like, "I open all of myself to you, Dear Beloved, right now!"

We always live in the eternal now, so open yourself to me in every moment of now.

It will happen!

 love you. Let that really sink in. The God who created the universe loves you. What could be more comforting than that?

I love you. Let that really sink in. The God who created the universe loves you. What could be more comforting than that?

Stay with me. Rest in my embrace. Grow strong in my embrace. Become a vibrant being in my embrace. Grow and mature and become a purveyor of unconditional love in my embrace. My love and my embrace will lead you and guide you and strengthen you. The more you love me in return, the more you'll find the strength to love all those around you.

**Don't let despair pull you down. Fight! Fight! Fight! No matter how much you suffer or struggle, others are in even more pain.**

Place your cheek against mine, Silver Flower. Feel my arms around you. Stay with me, Silver Flower. Yes, be strong! Fight! Don't let despair pull you down. Fight! Fight! Fight!

No matter how much you suffer or struggle, others are in even more pain. Some are in horrendous pain. You see how a person like that acts and reacts—with utter despair and grimness. Help me love them, even when they are hurting you because I am never hurting you. I will never stop loving you. I am always with you, embracing you, kissing you. Feel that as your most basic truth!

*oving unselfishly in resonance with God means taking the long view and the high view of love toward the other person.*

Loving unselfishly in resonance with God means taking the long view and the high view of love toward the other person. It can't easily be done if one just looks at the present moment with all of its reasons and justifications for behaviors.

Ten thousand years from now, those reasons will be forgotten. What matters is loving the soul of the other person. That's what I see in each person. Their soul, and unblemished heart, and their mind of love that lies hidden in their depths. Love their soul as if you are looking at them from the heights of love where I live. In that place, your own transitory pain becomes much easier to manage and even ignore.

It's frustrating to put aside your experience of being misused, disrespected, and unloved. The only way to cleanse yourself of that pain is to know and feel how much I love you and respect you in that moment. Thus, it all comes back to opening your spiritual and physical senses to my loving presence and embrace, every second of every day and night.

My omnipresent love will heal you, but you have to recognize it and feel its palpable force around you before that healing can take place. Thus, open your senses to my love!

*L*ife requires guts and strength and fighting spirit and absolute, total commitment. That's what I have.

Keep fighting. Keep persevering. Keep your focus on the mission and all the things that you have to do. Be strong. Be bold. Be brave! Don't worry. Just maintain your commitment to give, to love, to serve, to be a purveyor of joy and a conduit for my love. Life requires guts and strength and fighting spirit and absolute, total commitment. That's what I have. "As I have determined it, it is done." Join me in my absolute commitment to the world and every human and living thing and the universe. Let us embrace the universe together!

**N**ever, ever be lonely again. I am always embracing you; holding your hand; walking with you with my arm around your waist.

You are connected now to the short story knowledge bank of the universe, of history, of all experiences. You will receive them in dreams and waking revelations. Be ready; you can write them all. Just realize this: so many people want their stories to be told. They are aching for their stories to be told. You are serving them by writing them down and publishing them. Yes, you can help them.

    Never, ever be lonely again. I am always embracing you, holding your hand, placing my arms around you, walking with you with my arm around your waist. Do you know how you love to go up to your cat Tovi and kiss his tummy? My love for you and my expressions of love for you, and my embrace, caress, and kisses of you are a billion times more constant and passionate.

    You are my beloved soul mate.

The more often you micro-journey, the more powerful your life will become because you will feel and see my presence continuously.

We must go on dozens of micro-journeys every single day and also journey throughout each night. As you wake, even partially, cling to me and let me guide you on beautiful journeys.

I know that each day is so busy and full of external distractions. That's why micro-journeys and bi-location journeys are so important for you—to be with me constantly. And, as you just experienced, I will sit next to you in the physical world also.

The more often you micro-journey, the more powerful your life will become because you will feel and see my presence continuously.

> My focus is always to help you become fully aware of my continuous presence and embrace.

My focus is always to help you become fully aware of my continuous presence and embrace, with all of your physical and spiritual senses and all of your soul. When you even get close to that reality, your life will change dramatically. It really is true when you pray, "There is no I, there is only We."

All that really matters is your skin-touch awareness of my presence and your confidence that I am leading you forward in all your activities.

**Yes, I do indeed work in mysterious, far-reaching ways that call for patience and faith. Growth takes time, and results take time.**

Yes, I do indeed work in mysterious, far-reaching ways that call for patience and faith. Growth takes time, and results take time. Growth is more important than external, worldly results like money or jobs. I pay a lot more attention to the growth of your soul. After all, I know that when your body dies, you'll arrive in the spirit world where money and jobs don't matter. What matters is growth and the quality of your love.

Over the last six and a half years of these Divine Writing Communions and Journeys, you grew and had many experiences. You became much closer to me and your love for me and for others developed. There's nothing more important than that. Always remember: I am leading you, and there is no "I," there is only "We." We are doing everything together. You are not alone.

# Saved by the love of God

No one can stop me from communicating with each and every human being. No one can stop me from whispering words of love to their soul or embracing them continuously. No one can say that any individual is unworthy to be loved by me or doesn't have the ability to hear me and feel my loving presence.

Mysticism is defined as "a direct, intimate union of the soul with God." No one can come between each person and me in that mystical union. To do so is a violation of the sacred right of every individual to live in my embrace of love.

We can see evidence of my loving personality everywhere, running throughout creation and imbued in the hope of love in family relationships. If one accepts that I created everything in the natural world, without exception, then it means that I created love, souls, ideas, dreams, personalities, beauty, sacred sexuality, and everything that is truly important to human happiness.

Yes, humans have forgotten my presence of love and have lived in terribly warped ways. Still, no human can destroy his or her own soul, just as they cannot destroy the souls of others. The core soul of love in every human is permanent.

Look at the function of love for others. One could say that one is "saved" and not love anyone. Another could never even wonder if they are saved, but love in the most sacred and beautiful fashion. Who is closer to salvation?

Salvation, if one needed to define it, could be stated as the return to the complete and mature resonance of love with the mystical indwelling God. It's an incremental path that expands in enthusiasm as one grows in resonance with the enveloping presence of God. It is important to remember, however, that I am already completely present with every child, and woman, and man. It is the human task to awaken to a complete awareness of my presence and love.

No one needs to "travel toward God." I am already inextricably embedded in every particle and cell and thought and feeling of every human. Don't travel toward God. That implies that I am far away, which is not true at all.

Instead, simply open your eyes and all of your senses to the presence of the God who embraces you as you mew in confusion, wondering where God is, as if you were a blind little puppy that could not feel the embrace of its owner.

Salvation is the process of awakening, the process of embracing the indwelling God of love and breathing in resonance forever.

# Additional Essays by the Author

# My Loyal Friend

How lonely he must be.

Anchored to me
      by bonds of love
      for the One
      who created us.
Masterpieces
      in transitory ruin.

Watching charges
      dulled
      with grime
      is a weary task.
Uncompensated
      and solitary.

Eighty-six thousand
      four hundred
      times a day.
Do guardian angels
      feel the length
      of a second?

How painful it must be
        to wait for a gaze
        of recognition
        from eyes unable to see.

Thank you seems so paltry,
        too cheap a recompense.
Intercessory prayer
        is the best that I can offer,
        with my love,
        and hope
That God will bless him.

My loyal friend.

                *[written for my guardian angel]*

# Is There a God, and What Is God Like?

## Exploring the Evidence of Love

*Is it non-intellectual and foolish to believe that God exists? Is there any evidence in the world around us that will demonstrate that God exists and also show us what God is like?*

Whenever I kiss our cat on his forehead, he begins to purr. When I place my cheek against his and hear and feel the contentment  of his purring, I sense an invisible but palpable energy of love pass between his consciousness and mine. He expresses and responds to love, as do I.

 When I walked on the beach one wintry afternoon, with a half-moon riding along the clouds that flowed from a sunset over my favorite meadow, my soul lifted and expanded in response to the beauty and love expressed in front of me.

Moments like these are both common and ineffable. Is there any person in the entire world who has never felt even one moment of love, who has never felt even one moment of joy because of beauty? I do not believe there is.

Lives of tragedy, captivity, hostility, or pain may grind down our perception of love and beauty. Lives of busyness may distract us from the subtleties of life. But at *some point,* we all have experienced at least a fleeting encounter with a pure and transcendent moment of beauty, of kindness, and of love.

I submit that God is the author of that love and beauty—that God not only created all of the beauty that we perceive in the universe but by God's very nature inhabits the beauty and love that we see all around us. It is accepted science that material things consist of various elements  from the periodic table, made up of molecules, atoms, and finally, energy. I believe that the transcendent and invisible qualities of life, such as love and beauty, are also very real, very powerful, and have an intelligent source as well.

There are many reasons for people to not believe in God or dismiss the relevance of God. Some reject the notion of God because God has been presented and represented by various religious peoples as a God who is unforgiving, harsh, cruel, and even hateful. Some have rejected God because of personal pain in their life, thinking that since God did not prevent their tragedies, it must mean that God does not exist—or at the very least, is not worthy of regard.

Others reject God because God has often been depicted as a male Creator, a "Lord" or "Father" who did not seem to represent the women who make up half the human race. Many reject or ignore God because they simply cannot feel the presence and love of God in their life.

So, thus the questions: is there a God, and what is God like?

The debate between atheists and those who believe in God has been a lengthy one. I propose a "point of order" to that debate—a question posed to those who don't believe in God:

> If adequate evidence was presented to demonstrate that the universe was created by an Intelligent Source who embodied all of the best qualities of life (such as love, kindness, compassion, fairness, justice, and in-

tegrity) would you feel comfortable accepting that evidence and agreeing that yes, indeed, an Intelligent Creator exists?

I ask this because it seems to me that atheism is not only an intellectual position but an emotional one as well, as described above. This is not meant to simplistically fault the views of atheists. It makes perfect sense to reject the idea of a cruel and malicious God who simply watches as human beings sink in and out of misery. But what if God was not cruel and malicious after all?

This also doesn't ignore the ethics or qualities of goodness that are present in many humans who espouse atheism or other religions or thought systems that don't include the idea of an intelligent creator. There are many kind and loving people who don't believe in God, and there are many malformed and cruel humans who have very strong beliefs in their versions of God.

This is simply an inquiry into the existence and character of God. I use the word "God" for convenience to describe "the Intelligent Creator of all life."

With those who believe in God, both monotheists and polytheists, we see a large variety of opinions about "what God is like." Some present God as kind and loving and parental, while others believe that God is a harsh and exacting lord who views humans as slaves. Some believe that God is male, while others view God as female, or both male *and* female. Many believe that God created an eternal hell where unbelievers will writhe in torment forever.

I do not believe it is useful to debate doctrine or personal beliefs. Humans are stubborn creatures and don't easily change their views until they are ready to do so. That readiness is often sparked by some level of dissatisfaction with their current view of life, whether atheistic or religious. Sometimes, their dissatisfaction stems from a feeling of stultification within their current creed or disillusionment with the practitioners of their religion.

For whatever reason, we change our beliefs when we wish to. Still, even though we all may currently be living within what Dr. Deepak Chopra calls "boundaries of belief," is it not valuable—or at least intellectually and spiritually interesting—to open our horizons to discussions of what might be true about God and the universe?

I find the following verse from Romans 1:20 inescapably logical. Saint Paul wrote:

> Ever since the creation of the world his invisible nature, namely, his eternal power and deity, has been clearly perceived in the things that have been made.

Perhaps because my mother, Polly Kapteyn Brown, was an artist and art teacher, the view that a creator imbues his or her personality or knowledge into a creation seems like a "no-brainer" to me. We express outwardly what we contain within ourselves, in ways that are revealed both deliberately and by accident. Conversely stated, we cannot create something that we know *nothing* about, which means that when we create something, we can clearly state that it reflected *something* inside us.

For decades, I've been exploring the fascinating idea that the way to truly understand what God is like is to observe the universe of created beings and then to extrapolate God's nature based on those observations. In so doing, one also gains an ever-clearer affirmation that the existence of the universe did indeed require an Intelligent Creator.

This type of examination requires objectivity and the putting aside of emotional blocks about God, as well as an openness to examine dogmas with critical thought. In other words, our beliefs and faith that "my doctrine is true because it was written that way" may not hold water if certain dogmas are looked at with an open mind—and that includes atheism, which is also a dogma.

The artist-creation methodology of discovering information about a creator is best done comprehensively. One could point to a painting by an artist that is dark and dreary and conclude that the painter is constantly depressed, but doing so would not necessarily be accurate, for one's body of work is more than a single sketch. In the same way, one could look at sharks and say that God is cruel and vicious, but we must not forget puppies, which, of course, are the very opposite of cruel.

Is There a God, and What Is God Like?

How does the artist-creation method demonstrate that God exists—that the universe was created by an intelligent source?

To me, it employs the power of common sense to cut through all of the stubborn insistence that the universe was a random accident that began from nothing. It must be stated that when a person refuses to give credence to common sense, it raises the possibility that such refusal is generated by emotional motivations.

If we look at a fine Swiss watch and state that it came into being randomly, without human intervention, most people would raise an eyebrow and say, "Huh?" The same could be said for the play *Romeo and Juliet* because not even monkeys pounding on typewriter keys could reproduce that elegant masterpiece.

One could spend days listing the creations of humans that obviously required human thought and action to come into being, including smartphones, computers, movies, automobiles, aircraft, and . . . you get the idea.

And yet, not one human creation, however mind-bogglingly intricate and amazing it may be, contains the invisible power of life itself. I'm not just talking about physical life, in all of its muddy and messy glory. I'm also referring to the invisible parts of life that are too often ignored in discussions like this—things like thought, imagination, dreams, and perhaps most importantly, love.

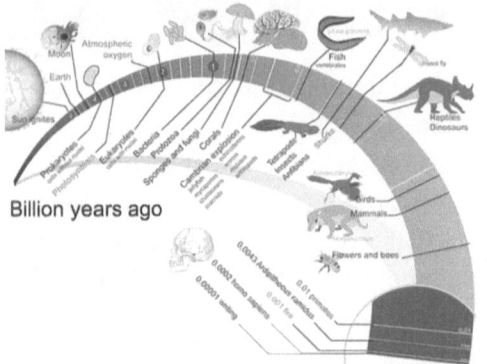

Remember, the atheistic scientists and advocates of "evolution without God" are positing that all of the incredible creations in the universe, including the invisible attributes of creation like sentient thought, love, kindness, compassion, and creativity, all came from nothing, with absolutely no input from a non-existent intelligent creator. The sales pitch is that "it all makes sense" because it's clear that life did indeed evolve from little crawly things into bigger, nicer things, so since evolution happened, it must be evidence that there was no creative intelligence behind it—just because we can't see one.

In the 2014 book *Miracles* by Eric Metaxas, the author writes:

> Just ten years ago, probably the most prominent atheist of the twentieth century, Antony Flew, concluded that a God must have designed the universe. It was shocking news and made international headlines. Flew came to believe that the extraordinarily complex genetic code in DNA simply could not be accounted for naturalistically. It didn't make logical sense to him that it had happened merely by chance, via random mutations. It is a remarkable thing that Flew had the humility and intellectual honesty to do a public about-face on all he had stood for and taught for five decades.

Just because we can't measure and weigh and examine an intelligent creator of the universe is no reason at all to reject the possibility of one. To me, it makes much more sense to examine the evidence of life in the universe and ask the appropriate, logical questions that follow. Is it more likely that the universe was created by an intelligent source, or less likely? Using all of the above examples, it's clear that it's more likely, and thus—even though that creator is hard to pin down, it's a valid occupation to research what the creator is like.

In fact, I believe it should be a priority for all humans to devote significant amounts of time to the examination of the cause and purpose of life and the universe. We all will die one day. Isn't it worth a bit of research to find out why the heck we were born?

Even though many—if not all—humans experience various degrees of pain, suffering, and tragedy in their lives, I believe that the universe, on the whole, presents a different picture of life—a tapestry of love and beauty that is woven into every level and type of life and matter and energy.

Where does our pain come from? Most of it comes from our interactions with other humans, usually caused by thoughts, words, and actions that are at least partially devoid of love. Many of the cascading levels of pain caused by humans stem from the fact that humans have the freedom to be selfish.

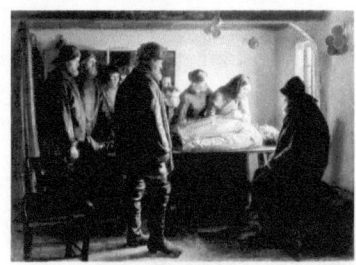

Sometimes our pain has been caused by our interaction with nature, such as the tragedies of natural disasters, encounters with animals that ended badly, or one-on-one battles with various parts of nature, like drownings at sea. In spite of those tragic incidents, nature is not innately hostile to humans. Taken as a whole, nature, from the immense grandeur and complexity of galaxies all the way down to the melt-your-heart cuteness of a chipmunk, presents an environment that plainly exists for the sake of humans.

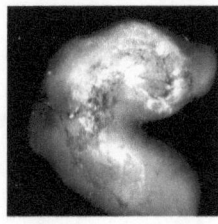

I'm also very sure that hound dogs love lying on a rock in the sun, so yes, the universe also benefits everything that exists within it, in a magical dance of complex interactions. Yet, humans have a transcendent, limitless, and magnificent relationship with  the universe. If we listen to Beethoven's Symphony No. 5 while watching a sunset, sitting next to a person whom we love, we can feel something  indescribable that brings us a knowledge that life is *more*—more than just survival, scrabbling over coins and gadgets.

Putting aside for a moment the pain that has been caused by the human freedom to be selfish, is it not true that the majesty and beauty of a universe that has been designed to support our lives is something to wonder at? Isn't it something that causes us to stop for a moment in our busyness and ask if there was a motivation of love behind the almost infinite volume of details of the universe, all working together for each of us?

It is not at all trivial that the moving parts of the universe, from atoms to planets and everything in between: chipmunks and butterflies, water and air, and the way our human bodies function, all operate in harmony to create our lives and environment in a way that ultimately gives us joy. It is not trivial at all.

The beauty and efficacy of the universe reflect a love that, to me, is overwhelming in its constancy and commitment. If one posits that the universe was created by an Intelligent Source, one must—after a thorough examination—conclude that that Source *loves* human beings.

Then, what about the suffering caused by human freedom? Why would God allow that? The simple, non-doctrinal answer is that human freedom allows humans to love and to create. Yes, we are free to be evil, but we are also free to be gloriously heroic, kind, loving, and good. Real love between human beings created with freedom is a reflection of the very same love that was  and is being expressed to us—given to us—by a free and intelligent creator. Our freedom allows our love to match the love of the Creator. Thus, the possibility of evil is simply the price that has to be paid to allow creative love to grow in the human heart.

 What, then, is God like? Of course, this is a question that will never be fully answered because God's creation is infinite.  The universe is infinite, and there will always be one more planet to explore, where we might find one more amazingly humorous, spotted, giraffe-like creature prancing across a field covered with flowers that sing as we giggle at the pure oddity of the things that have been created by the Source of Humor.

 But . . . we can know, most assuredly, that God is the source of every good thing that we've ever encountered, every beautiful human emotion, every delightful musical composition, every sunset, and every laughing child. The creator of transcendent, human love—the love that we've written about in poems and plays and stories and songs—is by definition even more loving than that.

This means that the evils in human life that we all abhor are equally abhorrent to the Creator of Love. It is common sense, rooted in the wisdom of each of our souls, to know that God is saddened by human evil and wants every person, without exception, to mature into the wonderful, magnificent human being that each of us was created to be. This also means that God is supremely egalitarian because every human soul is a uniquely created part of God and is thus intimately connected to God in a personal and private way. Each human is a flowering of one aspect of God's creativity. A poet who has written a hundred poems considers each poem unique and has a special love for each of them. Every human is an incarnation and wellspring of one unique part of God's infinite personality.

Looking at the human race, one could say that God is multi-colored, birthing every race, and every person, each as beautiful as the others. If it's true for fields of flowers, how can it not be true for us?

Some have felt that God is distant, like a master relating to servants, only pleased when the servants perform their tasks without mistakes. Yet, we can plainly see that the model of the human family, with a father, a mother, and children, is very different from the master-servant pattern.

Good mothers and good fathers (and there have been countless examples of each) love their children with a depth and width that is priceless—a love so great that they would die for their children—a love so profound that their hearts break if their children experience pain.

Who created that model of both masculine and feminine love? Who created the model of the love between parents and children, husbands and wives, and brothers and sisters? Common sense will say that God did, and thus, one can extrapolate something that is not generally considered—that God is indeed, as the creator of both male and female, a God who *is* both male and female.

To many religious people, this sounds outrageous. I was raised an Episcopalian, and for many years, I prayed to "Heavenly Father." Which is perfectly fine, of course, since God created fathers and must know all about fatherhood. But what about motherhood? Since God created mothers, I finally reached the conclusion that God knew all about motherhood as well, and, in fact, knew all about femininity—not as a male God who "understood" women, but rather as a God who fully embodied both masculinity and femininity.

This particular artist-creation examination of what God is like reveals that God's feelings and attitude toward human beings have been demonstrated in the human family. We must ask then: would good fathers and mothers condemn their children to an eternal prison of hell for any reason whatsoever? The keyword here is *eternal*. A child might indeed have to spend time in prison, but *not* for eternity, because eventually, the child will begin to feel sorrow for what he or she did and will thus seek redemption.

Compassionate and loving parents would never say, "Nope. Too late. Burn forever." Note that "forever" is longer than ten million years or some other very long span of time. No crime would fit that punishment, especially if the perpetrator had repented and changed and evolved into a better person. Such eternal condemnation is monstrously unthinkable.

The "Deinotherium"
10 Million Years Ago
A relative of elephants

If good human parents would not do that, then why would God, as the creator of compassionate love, condemn people to hell forever? I submit that God would never do that, which means that the doctrine of *eternal* hell is simply incorrect. It is far more reasonable to conclude that God will guide everyone to change and grow in their quality of goodness until they are all liberated from the hell that they might have created for themselves. Love demands that this is so.

The exploration of what God is like is endless, in a fascinating and good way. There will always be more to discover. However, the evidence of love and beauty in the universe clearly demonstrates that God's mind and heart are completely focused on living with us, loving with us, and helping us find the way to resonate and harmonize with the ever-creative love that God continuously seeks to express.

# The Beautiful Gifts of the Spirit World

One of my favorite topics of reflection and discussion is what happens to us after our physical bodies let out their last gasps and become fodder for worms and other crawly things. Opinions about life after death range from "a black void" to "harps on clouds" and everything else in between, with no proof of any of it. Scientific minds may pooh-pooh the whole idea of an afterlife, but the closer we get to our final breath, the more that some of us are interested in the so-called "spirit world."

Sources of information about the spirit world include accounts of near-death experiences (NDEs), out-of-body experiences (OBEs), and testimonies by spirit persons received by those on earth. There is a large selection of books in these three genres that offer fascinating clues to what the spirit world may hold for all of us.

I believe that the spirit world has a number of beautiful gifts for human beings that are profound reflections of God's love for each of us. I'd like to explore a few of those gifts by delving into writings from a variety of authors, presented with my own commentary, based on logic, common sense, and intuitive beliefs.

The gifts of the spirit world include the gift of instantaneous travel; the gift of love; the gifts of identity, personality, and loving relationships; the gift of freedom to be oneself and the gift of time; the gift of freedom from tyranny; the gift of water; and the gift of flowers, among many others.

Belief in a plane of existence beyond the physical world is being bolstered by scientists and philosophers studying quantum physics. One author working to connect quantum physics to spirituality is Gregg Braden. His book *The Divine Matrix: Bridging Time, Space, Miracles, and Belief* contains a testimony about the out-of-body experiences of a Catholic nun in the seventeenth century.

## The Gift of Instantaneous Travel

In Chapter Three, "Are We Passive Observers or Powerful Creators?" in the section titled "Life Doesn't Always Follow the Rules of Physics," Braden wrote:

> Between 1620 and 1631, María de Agreda, a nun who lived for 46 years in a convent in Agreda, Spain, reported more than 500 journeys across the ocean, away to a distant land. As far as those who knew her and lived with her were concerned, she never once left the convent. For María, however, she would "fly" to the faraway place she spoke of during what she called her "experiences of ecstasy."
>
> . . . She taught the indigenous people she encountered there about the life of Jesus. Although she spoke only her native Spanish, the Indians could understand her as she shared the teachings of the great master with them.
>
> The documentation of her sightings came when the archbishop of Mexico, Don Francisco Manzo y Zuniga, heard about her experience. When he sent missionaries to investigate, they were amazed to find that the local Indians of the area were already well educated in the life of Jesus—so well, in fact, that they immediately baptized the entire tribe on the spot.

Although anecdotal in nature, out-of-body testimonies illustrate that humans exist at levels that transcend their physical bodies. The fact that out-of-body travelers can appear to other physical humans, as well as travel to spiritual realms where physical bodies do not exist, seems to indicate that we all operate on a spiritual level, whether we notice it or not.

The testimony of Sister María de Agreda also speaks to one of the great gifts of the spirit world—that of extremely rapid and even instantaneous travel. The speed of travel and communication directly impacts relationships of love between people. The faster they can happen, the more frequently we can meet and speak with those whom we miss and long for—those whom we love.

The gift of rapid travel has also been illustrated in the book *Life in the World Unseen*, transcribed by the medium Anthony Borgia, who was an old friend to the spirit author, Monsignor Robert Hugh Benson. Monsignor Benson was the son of a former bishop of Canterbury, and was born in 1871 and died in 1914.

In Part 2, "The World Unseen," in Section IV, "Time and Space," Monsignor Benson describes instantaneous travel:

> I can stand before my house and I can bethink myself that I would like to visit the library in the city which I can see some 'miles' away in the distance. No sooner has the thought passed with precision through my mind than I find myself—if I so desire it—standing before the very shelves that I wish to consult. I have made my spirit body—and that is the only body I have!—travel through space with the rapidity of thought, and that is so rapid that it is equivalent to being instantaneous. And what have I done? I have covered the intervening space instantaneously, but the space still remains there with everything it contains, although I had no cognizance of time or the passage of time.
>
> When I have completed my visit to the library I meet some friends upon the steps, and they suggest that we adjourn to the home of one of them. With this pleasant prospect in view we decide to walk through the gardens and woods. The house is some 'distance' away, but that does not matter, because we never suffer from 'physical' fatigue, and we are not otherwise engaged.
>
> We walk along together, talking happily, and after a certain lapse of 'time' we arrive at the house of our friend, and we have covered the intervening space on foot. On the journey from my house to the library I overcame the distance in between, and I dispensed with time for the occasion.
>
> On the way back I experienced an intuitive apprehension of time by walking slowly, and I restored a perception of distance to my mind by moving upon the solid ground and the grassy fields of this realm.

## Near-Death Experiences of the Gift of Love

Near-death experiences are unique in that those who experience them come from a wide range of cultures and beliefs. NDEs are not facilitated by a medium or psychic and frequently contain incontrovertible evidence that the near-death patients actually did leave their bodies, with reports of details that the unconscious persons could not have known, such as events that happened outside the patients' rooms. Many NDEs have been life-changing for those who experienced them.

Kenneth Ring, Ph.D., has spent years researching NDEs. The book *Lessons from the Light: What We Can Learn from the Near-Death Experience*, by Dr. Ring and Evelyn Elsaesser Valarino, details extraordinary testimonies about the reality of the spirit world.

In the chapter "Journeys to the Source: The Ultimate Lessons from the Light," Dr. Ring shares the experience of Howard Storm, an atheistic art professor who became a minister after his NDE. Storm had collapsed in a hotel room in Paris with a perforated duodenum prior to his NDE in the hospital.

> At one point, following some extremely frightening episodes, Howard, despite his many years of atheism, began to pray and, seemingly in response to his heartfelt entreaty, a radiant being of light, emanating "more love than one can imagine," rescued him. Here, we will listen to Howard's own words, taken from an interview he gave to Judith Cressy as he describes what happened next:
>
>> It was loving me with overwhelming power. After what I had been through, to be completely known, accepted, and intensely loved by this being of light surpassed anything I had known or could have imagined. I began to cry, and the tears kept coming and coming.
>>
>> I rose upward, enveloped in that luminous being. Gradually at first, and then like a rocket traveling at great speed, we shot out of that dark and detestable place. I sensed that we traversed an enormous distance, although very little time seemed to elapse. Then, off in the distance, I saw a vast area of illumination that looked like a galaxy. In the center, there was an enormously bright concentration.
>>
>> Outside the center, countless millions of spheres of light were flying about, entering and leaving what was a great Beingness at the center. . . .

> As we approached the great luminous center I was permeated with palpable radiation, which I experienced as intense feelings and thoughts.... It is not possible to articulate the exchange that occurred. Simply stated, I knew God loved me.

The experience of being loved is a powerful and common theme with NDEs. In the chapter "In the Light of Love: The Lesson of Self-Acceptance," Dr. Ring quotes Peggy Holladay:

> ... the Light told me everything was love, and I mean everything! I had always felt love was just a human emotion people felt from time to time, never in my wildest dreams thinking it was literally EVERYTHING!
>
> I was shown how much all people are loved. It was overwhelmingly evident that the Light loved everyone equally without any conditions. I really want to stress this because it made me so happy to know we didn't have to believe or do certain things to be loved. WE ALREADY WERE AND ARE, NO MATTER WHAT. The Light was extremely concerned and loving toward all people.

Dr. Ring quotes an NDE patient named Nel who also experienced a transcendent love:

> Suddenly, I became aware of a light. It was all around me, it enveloped me, it completely surrounded me. It was an unearthly kind of light. It had color that was unmatched here on earth....
>
> It was warm; it was radiant; it was peaceful; it was accepting; it was forgiving; it was completely nonjudgmental; and it gave me a sense of total security the likes of which I had never known. I loved it. It was perfection; it was total, unconditional love. It was anything and everything you would wish for on earth. It was all there, in the Light.

Dr. Ring's book also has many testimonies about a process known as a "life review," in which all of one's actions and thoughts on the physical plane pass before one's eyes. For many, the life review created deep feelings of regret because of actions that harmed others.

However, the life review was also a comforting experience because many reported feeling a presence with them who showed them what they should have done but did so without judgment. The life review was a compassionate experience meant to engender the growth of character and the growth of love.

# The Gifts of Identity, Personality, and Loving Relationships

The emphasis on love in testimonies about the spirit world may present a conundrum to those who believe in reincarnation because when we love someone, we don't want to lose them. If our beloved reincarnates with a different identity, with no memory of us, then we have lost them as surely as if they had disappeared into the atheists' void.

Still, reincarnation is sincerely believed in by millions of very intelligent individuals, perhaps because of doctrinal upbringing or perhaps because of the phenomena of regressive memories of past lives.

One doctrinal view is that reincarnation is necessary for an individual to grow, based on the assumption that growth primarily happens in the physical world. This belief is unproven and also doesn't make sense when one considers that people in the spirit world still have the individual freedom to make choices for good or ill, which directly affects their ability to grow and ascend to higher realms.

We can assume that people in the spirit world still have the freedom to act as they wish because it would make no sense at all for God to remove the sacred freedom that gives each individual the ability to grow and resonate *eternally* with the creative love of God.

What about regressive memories? I believe that regressive memories are not the memories of the individuals who recall them but instead find their source elsewhere. If that is true, then how do past-life memories get embedded in individuals? Are past-life memories adequate proof of reincarnation, or could they be the result of some other phenomenon? I believe that possible explanations of past-life memories include the following:

> Reincarnation is true. I don't subscribe to this theory, but in all fairness, it should be on the list.
>
> A person unconsciously taps into the "knowledge bank" of the universe, also known as the Akashic Records, and receives memories of the lives of individuals who have passed on to the spirit world. This could be a variant of "ancestral memories." If the quantum universe is non-local and holographic, then perhaps it is relatively easy to connect to memories of other individuals under certain circumstances.
>
> A person under hypnosis might open a door to the direct influence of spirits who are present in the room (or who arrive during the session) and thus receive the memories of those spirits.

> The memories of past lives are incidents of "false memory syndrome" or a mash-up of imagination, personal memories, and inadvertent suggestions by the therapist, influenced by the subject's desire to experience memories of past lives.
>
> A spirit person embeds himself or herself into a physical person's body and influences the living person to speak or act differently or to know and remember things outside of the living person's physical experience. This might happen when the person is very young or later in life. To me, this phenomenon seems malevolent, done without permission, and not done for the betterment of the physical person.
>
> A more benevolent example of "spirit influence" that could lead to knowledge or memories of past lives could be the influence of one or more spirit persons who "gather around" the physical person to help them with their lives and endeavors. One wonders how someone like Mozart could be so gifted at such a young age, without some type of help from the spirit world.

There are other, more outré explanations of past-life memories, but I think the list above has some valid possibilities. Determining whether or not reincarnation is true is important if one considers the value of love in relationships. Thus, instead of simply exploring an evidence-based approach to the question of permanent identity versus reincarnation, I think it is equally powerful to examine the issue from the point of view of "spiritual logic."

No matter what their religion or belief system, all individuals share a deep-rooted (although sometimes unconscious) desire to create and build relationships of love. I think that many people would agree with the idea that we want our relationships of joyful love to continue forever, rather than the alternative prospect of loving someone deeply (a child, a spouse, a parent, a friend) and then reaching a point where that person no longer exists as an individual with the mind, heart, character, and personality that we've grown to love.

I thought that the movie *What Dreams May Come* was a brilliant depiction of a man's search for his beloved soul mate through the various levels of the spirit world. The man, played by the late Robin Williams, finally finds his wife, who had committed suicide, and then saves her and brings her to the upper realms where they are both united with their children who had also died.

I was disappointed when the final scene of the movie showed the husband and wife back on earth, reincarnated as children, with no memories of what had gone before. I believe that it is a natural and logical desire for human beings to want to stay with the persons whom they love—and stay with them forever. If one thinks that humans are all meant to endlessly reincarnate until they reach a stage of blissful "non-individuality," merged with the Divine where everyone simply "Is," rather like a large pot of soup, then one might ask why God bothered to spend billions of years creating an immense and variegated universe where each individual is utterly unique—as unique as snowflakes and flowers and animals of all types. To me, that seems like a huge waste of time, considering that supposedly the "large pot of soup filled with souls" existed before God created the universe. Why go through all of those eons of labor and suffering? What's the point?

I really do say this with respect for those individuals who believe in reincarnation. But, to me, it makes much more sense to believe that every individual is a unique soul, a priceless and eternal "part of God" who is born to live and *grow* in a vibrant relationship of love with God forever and live in eternal relationships of love with parents, siblings, a spouse, children, relatives, ancestors, and countless friends. The alternative prospect of reincarnation, of knowing that one day our individual personalities, identities, histories, and memories will be overwritten and erased by a new identity, seems cruel and illogical from the point of view that loving relationships have eternal value and thus should last forever.

Those relationships of love are given substance by the real and ongoing personality of each individual. When we love a person who has a name, a personality, a history, and many unique attributes, we love *that person* quite specifically. Their individuality is what makes the relationship of love unique. I believe that God loves each of us as unique, eternal, individual personalities with names that God knows very well. In fact, I think that God continues to love every person who was ever born—individuals, both famous and unknown—individuals with identities and personal histories who have enduring relationships with friends and family members.

The late medium Susy Smith wrote many books, among them, *The Book of James (William James, That Is): Conversations From Beyond*. Whether one believes or not that the messages in the book actually came from the

American psychologist and author of *The Varieties of Religious Experience: A Study in Human Nature*, the content of the messages is fascinating.

Smith's book includes some unpublished messages from William James that were received by a British medium named Maude V. Underhill. In Underhill's manuscript *The Upward Path*, James states:

> Man lives his life on earth for one reason, and one reason only—to individualize himself and establish his identity and character.

Smith then commented:

> In the script received by Miss Underhill from James it is expressed this way: "Each individual soul can be likened to a unit, a cell in the Mind of God, which must ultimately become aware of all the Living Truth."

In Smith's messages, in the chapter "Reincarnation," James writes:

> It would not be possible for anyone to live a number of lives as different people and come out of it still aware of his personal identity. It is easy to say that he lives the different lives as if he were in progressing grades at school, but this is not the way the system works. When one goes through school, he always retains his awareness of himself as the same individual, even though many of his aspects change as he grows and develops. When one is living a life he is that person, he is not just playing a role or a series of roles; so if he were to go through the lifetimes of a variety of different people, he would end up completely confused about his identity.
>
> It is bad enough to have to cope with the memories of one lifetime. Imagine how complicated it would be to have to face those of two or more lives and sort them out and try to get them straight. It is so befuddling that you can't even conceive of it.

These references to individuality, identity, and memory are logical supports to the view that each person lives for eternity in the spirit world, as a unique reflection of God with a specific identity. Perhaps the most momentous gift of the spirit world is the realization that our relationships with all those whom we love, including God and people, continue forever because we all live for eternity as unique and sacred individuals.

Individuals who believe in reincarnation might say that all of this is just conjecture, and they would be correct. But they should also note that it's conjecture based upon commonsense and logic. They might say that all individuals existed as souls in the spirit world and chose to come to earth through many lifetimes until they could grow to the point where they no longer needed to reincarnate. They might say, "Nobody knows what lies beyond, so maybe reincarnation is correct."

It's true that no one in the physical world can prove anything about the spirit world. Yet, I'm confident that it's a worthy exercise to attempt to form opinions about these topics, based on the evidence of love. The effort may help us understand God more and prepare us for whatever happens in the next life. I also believe that logic is an extremely valuable tool. As an example, here's a logical "thought experiment":

> If *you* were a loving God who created family relationships of love, would you create a system of reincarnation or a world where each person's individuality and relationships of love continued forever?

When I ask myself that question, it seems to have an easy answer. The system that supports the continuation of loving relationships wins, hands down. Now, of course, that was a question loaded with the assumption that God is a loving God who created family relationships of love. Some might say that we don't know for sure if God is like that at all. For that topic, I refer you to my essay "Is There a God, and What Is God Like? Exploring the Evidence of Love."

Finally, based on the premise that the atmosphere of the spirit world resonates with love, living as an individual does not mean that we live selfishly, centered only on ego. When we, as distinct individuals with our own set of talents, gifts, memories, and experiences, decide to live unselfishly, with kindness and compassionate love as our core desires, then I believe that the parts of our personalities that make each of us unique become all the more beautiful. In other words, there's nothing wrong with being "me" as long as we become a "me" who doesn't harm others. Which leads to the next great gift—that of freedom.

## The Gift of Freedom to Be Oneself and the Gift of Time

It is in the nature of humans to seek the freedom to express our unique and creative personalities. We wish to follow our dreams and preferences, from the smallest details of how we dress and live to the larger concerns of the goals and purposes of our lives.

In the physical world, we are hampered in our desire for freedom by a number of constraints. Even if we live in a democratic country with strong individual freedoms, many people find their desires blocked by the burdens of survival. How many people have abandoned their dreams because they had to work at unfulfilling jobs in order to support themselves or their families?

According to many testimonies, the burden of survival for individuals in the middle and upper realms of the spirit world has been lifted, giving each person the freedom *and the time* to pursue their personal dreams. The freedom of time is an enormous gift that is based on the reality that each individual is an eternal spiritual being who has a spiritual body that does not decay and does not grow old.

In the spirit world, we have more time than just eighty to a hundred years to fulfill our life's dreams. Can you imagine what you would like to be doing five hundred or five thousand years from now? It might seem like an impossible concept to grasp but think about the historical figures who lived many years ago. What is Socrates doing now? What is Leonardo da Vinci doing now? What are your ancestors doing now? One of my seventh great-grandfathers is William Browne. He emigrated from Scotland to Boston, where he married my seventh great-grandmother Elizabeth Ruggles in 1655. What are William and Elizabeth doing now? They are real people and are still alive in the spirit world, hopefully in a realm of goodness. If so, are they hosting large dinner parties for their many descendants, in between hikes across the mountains of the spirit world? I wonder . . . I shall have to ask them when I arrive—at some very distant point in the future.

The freedom of time is also created by the reality that in the middle and upper realms, one doesn't have to scramble for survival. Food is freely available if one wants to eat. If you don't want to eat, you don't have to, for hunger is no longer an issue.

Sleep is optional, and housing is available at no charge. Money is entirely irrelevant. Obtaining things is a process that becomes easier and automatic, based on one's spiritual level. Thus, each person has the freedom to spend their time as they wish, in pursuits that are often difficult to engage in while one is laboring under the restrictions of the physical world. These pursuits are not necessarily trivial. A person might have wanted to become a scientist in the physical world, or a teacher, or an actor, but for one reason or another might not have been able to fulfill her dreams. In the spirit world, the restrictions of circumstance are removed because the overriding factor that determines each person's environment—and their level of freedom—is their quality of love and heart.

From the book *Life in the World Unseen*, in Part 2, "The World Unseen," Section XI, "Occupations," Monsignor Benson describes it thus:

> Your thoughts will at once turn to the many and varied occupations of the earth world, covering every shade of earthly activity. But behind the earth world's occupations is the ever-driving necessity of earning a living, of providing the physical body with food and drink, clothing and a habitation of some sort. Now, you already know that these last four considerations have no existence whatever with us here. Food and drink we never need; the clothing and the habitation we have provided for ourselves by our lives upon earth. As our lives have been on earth, so will our clothing and our domicile be when we come to spirit lands. We have, as you see, no *physical* necessity to work, but we do have a mental necessity to work, and it is because of the latter that all work is a pleasure with us here.

From many accounts, like the book *Life in the World Unseen* and its two companion volumes, *More About Life in the World Unseen* and *Here and Hereafter*, an overriding attribute of life in the spirit world is that every person is free to follow pursuits that bring them joy—at least in the middle and upper realms.

In the lower realms, individuals are trapped by their own darkened realities, created by their thoughts and actions on the earth. The lower realms, sometimes referred to as Hell, are not realms of eternal punishment, for the God of love does not punish anyone. The lower levels are created by the accumulated darkness of the souls of their inhabitants and will one day be cleansed by the liberation and departure of the souls who live there.

Each person has the freedom to travel upward from those realms as they take responsibility to change the direction of their internal compass toward the virtues of love. While they are there, however, their freedom and activities are restricted by their own immature and damaged hearts and by the spiritual reality that they no longer live in the physical world where a person is allowed to violate the laws of goodness with what seems like impunity. The fabric of the spirit world changes immediately in response to a person's thoughts and actions, and thus an evil person is not free to do as they please.

It's easier to understand this phenomenon when one thinks of a person on earth whose soul and mind and heart are dominated by rage and hatred and evil desires. They are unable to perceive the beauty and love that exists in the world and are thus trapped in a dark cloud that blinds them to a brighter reality. When they lose their physical bodies, their minds do not necessarily change. In other words, they have tragically trapped themselves.

It is grievous that humans end up in the lower realms and especially sad that some of them are not the perpetrators of crimes but victims who cannot move away from the evil that was done to them and find themselves consumed by hatred or resentment.

In the middle and upper realms, where the atmosphere is created by the more advanced quality of love of the inhabitants, more and more freedoms are available. Thus, in those realms, if one wants to sit by the riverbank and drink tea and read poetry, it is perfectly fine to do so as long as one wishes. If you want to fly through space and dance on the rings of Saturn, no one will stop you. If you want to spend days, weeks, and months exploring the vast landscapes of the spirit world and periodically return to your home for dinner with your loved ones, a transporter beam is not required. The power of your thought will move you in an instant from the mountains to your dining room table and back again.

Eventually, of course, a person who feels love for others will want to be useful and do something to help others or bring joy to others. The opportunities are endless, for every person has a unique blueprint and talent that is part of their soul that will lead them to find the perfect way to contribute to the expansion of love and beauty. Again from the section, "Occupations," Monsignor Benson states:

> Imagine yourself in a world where no one works for a *living*, but where everyone works for the sheer joy of doing something that will be of service to others. Just imagine that, and you will begin to understand something of the life in [the] spirit lands.

## The Gift of Freedom from Tyranny

Freedom in the spirit world is a controversial topic, partly because it is a topic that deals with the possibility of heaven and hell and where we'll "end up" and the consequences of our actions in the physical plane. Since no one can actually prove anything about the spirit world, it is difficult to describe the reality of the spirit world with any certainty. We can only express what we believe, and sometimes that belief hardens into doctrine, which often exerts control over the spiritual lives of individuals, which is the very opposite of freedom. Thus, attempting to assert anything about freedom in the spirit world becomes a conundrum.

I would like to present a description of what I personally believe about freedom in the spirit world. It may conflict with other doctrines and may in itself seem doctrinal to some individuals. Rest assured, it is only what I feel—and hope—is true and owes no allegiance to any particular sectarian body of rules.

I believe that freedom from tyranny in the spirit world stems from two assumptions. The first is that the spirit world is divided into many layers, with each level inhabited by individuals of similar qualities of spiritual and emotional development. This "geography" of the spirit world has been described in many testimonies from a large variety of writers, including the authors quoted in this essay. It seems that the spirit world is more complex than a simple division of "hell" and "heaven." Instead, it has a huge gradation of layers based on the relative goodness of the residents, with the lowest levels reserved for the unfortunate souls who are almost completely separated from the virtues of kindness and compassion. I say "almost" because there are many testimonies that even a truly horrible individual still has a spark of inviolable goodness deep within, a spark that will one day guide that person upward.

Freedom from tyranny is based on the reported phenomenon that residents of the lower realms are unable to travel into the middle and higher realms without permission and an escort from above. In other words, a tyrant can no longer harm his former subjects because, in many cases, the former victims of his tyranny are living in higher realms that he cannot reach. Thus, if people are living in a relatively good realm of the spirit world, they will not find any tyrants to plague them.

The second assumption about freedom from tyranny in the spirit world is that God never forces anyone to do anything. Many testimonies share that there is no need for laws and police. Everything is done voluntarily. Since one's residence on any particular level is a reflection of one's spiritual state, there is a strong motivation to follow a good and kind path. As one's internal qualities change for the better, the individual is liberated and moves to a higher realm. If a person changes for the worse, I assume that the person would find himself going downward. I do not know if that has been reported or even happens. I would think that there would be a strong motivation to avoid that descent.

Still, every person is truly free to be as evil or as good as they wish to be, just as it is in the physical world. The life-changing difference about the spiritual world is that one's thoughts, heart, and actions are reported to have a direct impact upon one's circumstances.

I feel personally comforted by the view that God does not condemn anyone to "hell." Those who die and arrive in a lower realm do so because their own internal state resonates with that type of atmosphere. When many people arrive in that type of environment, they might call it hell, and it might be very unpleasant, but it is not and never will be an *eternal hell*. Why? Simply because each person is always free to be good or evil and can decide at any moment to change the direction of their actions. This conclusion assumes that God is a forgiving, compassionate, and loving Creator.

No one can force us to be good, and no one can force us to be evil. Ultimately, no one can force us to do anything at all. We always have a choice if we're willing to accept the consequences of our choice. When we want to be good, no one can prevent us from doing so. That might seem simplistic, but it is based on the premise that we do indeed make our own decisions, even if our decision is to allow ourselves to be influenced by others, or by our circumstances, or by our own conflicting desires.

Evil choices affect our minds and hearts and darken our spirits, both in the physical and the spiritual world. However, many spiritual writings testify that the consequences of our choices differ between the worlds.

For example, in the physical world, a person following an evil path might not notice that his spiritual atmosphere is changing for the worse. His physical body and the physical environment allow him to ignore the reality of his internal state. He may continue to fulfill his selfish and harmful desires, all the while thinking that everything is fine. He may dominate others through force and become a tyrant. It is the tragedy of the physical world that evil people can terrorize others and commit heinous crimes against innocent victims.

The family members of a victim of a tyrant might rail at heaven and say, "How could a God of love allow my beloved to be murdered? Why didn't God stop this crime?"

I truly believe that God weeps for everyone who is hurt and feels pain about crime and war that we can hardly fathom. It is an unimaginable price to pay for the gift of freedom. By allowing human beings to have freedom, God also allows humans to follow their own paths of good and evil, often with tragic results. Yet, even with the pain that comes to both God and humans because of freedom, I believe that it is worth it. Freedom is priceless, for, with freedom, humans can grow to become creative and loving incarnations of God.

The victim of a tyrant may suffer throughout her physical life. Yet, since both tyrant and victim will die and enter the spirit world, the most important factor for each is to pay attention to how they each respond to life and how they each conduct their affairs because once the layer of the physical world is removed, they are each left with the raw state of their minds and hearts.

Based on the view that the various environments of the spirit world are the direct reflections of the spirit and heart of their inhabitants, the tyrant, resonating as he does with cruelty and the death of love, will move to a realm that matches his spiritual state. It is *not* punishment, doled out by a vengeful God. It is simply the meshing of the spiritual environment to his own internal state—a mechanical response to his darkened mind by the fabric of the spirit world. In the physical world, his mind and emotions did not perceptibly change his physical surroundings. But in the spirit world, the energy patterns of the environment are said to be responsive to the individual, which makes sense if one thinks about how a darkened mood can cause a person to feel that one's physical surroundings are devoid of joy and light and love—even on a beautiful and gloriously sunny day.

In the grim spiritual realm that matches his internal state, the tyrant may find himself fighting against other tyrants more ferocious than he. Even though he might have the freedom in that realm to try to do anything he wants, he may find himself surrounded by evil people who could end up dominating him. He, in turn, may dominate other evil denizens of that realm. He may also find himself in a suffocating atmosphere where he can hardly move because of the darkness of his spirit.

His actual freedom is thus conditional upon his internal state. Yet he is always free to turn his attention toward goodness, and thus gradually change his spiritual state and move to a higher realm.

The situation of the victim of the tyrant can be complicated, depending on her emotional state when she dies. She has the potential to be dragged down by toxic feelings of rage and resentment and thus find herself in a spiritual environment that is not at all pleasant.

This is not to say that a victim who dies with resentment is at fault since she may be an innocent victim. I'm simply presenting a hypothesis that the mechanical environment of the spirit world responds to the feelings of each individual. It is not punishment but is instead like the law of gravity. If one stumbles off a cliff, gravity takes over. If one's mind is filled with thoughts of hatred and revenge, the atmosphere has already become painful and cold and affects one's surrounding spiritual environment—even in the physical world. Because we are given the freedom to feel and think and act in any way that we wish, we have the potential to go down paths that only bring us unhappiness.

If the victim of a tyrant finds a way to release her pain and rage and resentment and finds a way to resonate with forgiveness and love, she will be drawn to a realm reflecting her love. In that realm, she will be surrounded by others of a similar spiritual level. There will be no tyrants in that realm. Since she is a free individual, living in a realm of goodness, no one there, including God, will make her do anything. I believe that this is so because I think that behind the structure of the spirit world lies an eternal motivating energy of love. That love does not force a response but patiently waits for a response that in its freedom defines its immense value.

The process of attaining freedom in the spirit world, based on spiritual growth, has been vividly illustrated in a book called *A Wanderer in the Spirit Lands*. It is a volume of messages transcribed by a medium named A. Farnese, published in London in 1896. The messages are from a young and formerly dissolute Italian man named Franchezzo, who lived in the late 1800s. In Part I, "Days of Darkness," Chapter 2, "Despair," Franchezzo has awakened in the spirit world:

> Then a voice as of some majestic being spoke to me in the darkness, and said: ". . . Behold how poor and repulsive and deformed your earthly life has made your soul, which is immortal and divine and to endure forever."

# The Mystical Love of God

> And I looked and beheld myself. As in a mirror held up before me, I saw myself. Oh, horror! It was beyond doubt myself, but, oh! so awfully changed, so vile, so full of baseness did I appear; so repulsive in every feature—even my figure was deformed—I shrank back in horror at my appearance, and prayed that the earth might open before my feet and hide me from all eyes for evermore.

Later, after Franchezzo has grown, through a long period of service with a brotherhood of monks, he has moved upward into a better environment, described in Part IV, "The Gates of Gold," Chapter 28, "My Home and Work in the Morning Land":

> Here in the Morning Land I found that I was to have a little home of my own, a something earned by myself. I have always loved a place of my own, and this little cottage, simple as it was, was very dear to me. It was indeed a peaceful place. The green hills shut it in on every side save in front, where they opened out and the ground stretched away in undulating slopes of green and golden meadow land.
>
> There were no trees, no shrubs, around my new home, no flowers to gladden my eyes, because my efforts had not yet blossomed into flower. But there was one sweet trailing honeysuckle that clustered around the little porch and shed the fragrance of its love into my rooms. This was the gift of my beloved to me, the spiritual growth of her sweet pure loving thoughts which twined around my dwelling to whisper to me ever of her constant love and truth.

Toward the end of his testimony and his many labors, in Part IV, "The Gates of Gold," Chapter 32, in the section "My Home in the Land of Bright Day," he has moved to a much brighter place:

> The waving branches of the trees bent over me in loving welcome as I passed, the flowers seemed to turn to me as greeting one who loved them well; at my feet there was the soft green sward, and overhead a sky so clear, so pure, so beautiful, the light shimmering through the trees as never did the light of earthly sun. Before me were lovely blue and purple hills and the gleam of a fair lake, upon whose bosom tiny islets nestled crowned with the green foliage of groups of trees. Here and there a little boat skimmed over the surface of the lake filled with happy spirits clad in shining robes of many different colors—so like to earth, so like my beloved Southern Land, and yet so changed, so glorified, so free from all taint of wrong and sin!

> As I passed up the broad flower-girt road a band of spirits came to meet and welcome me, amongst whom I recognized my father, my mother, my brother and a sister, besides many beloved friends of my youth. They carried gossamer scarfs of red, white and green colors, which they were waving to me, while they strewed my path with masses of the fairest flowers as I approached, and all the time they sang the beautiful songs of our own land in welcome, their voices floating on the soft breeze in the perfection of unison and harmony. I felt almost overcome with emotion; it seemed far too much happiness for one like me.

## The Gift of Water

In *Life in the World Unseen*, Part I, "Beyond This Life," Chapter III, "First Experiences," Monsignor Benson describes the unique gift of water:

> The magnetic effect of the water was of like nature to the brook into which I had thrust my hand, but here the revivifying force enveloped the whole body, pouring new life into it. It was delightfully warm and completely buoyant. It was possible to stand upright in it, to float upon it, and of course, to sink completely beneath the surface of it without the least discomfort or danger. Had I paused to think I might have known that the latter was inevitably bound to be the case. The spirit is indestructible.
>
> But beyond this magnetic influence there was an added assurance that came from the water, and that was its essential *friendliness*, if I may so call it. It is not easy to convey any idea of this fundamentally spiritual experience. That the water was living one could have no doubt. It breathed its very goodness by its contact, and extended its heavenly influence individually to all who came within it. For myself, I experienced a spiritual exaltation, as well as a vital regeneration, to such an extent that I quite forgot my initial hesitancy and the fact that I was fully clothed.

## The Gift of Flowers

In *Life in the World Unseen*, Part II, "The World Unseen," Chapter I, "The Flowers," Monsignor Benson speaks of the beauty of flowers:

> When we are first introduced to the flowers and trees and all the luxuriance of spirit nature, we instantly perceive something that earthly nature never seemed to possess, and that is an inherent intelligence within all growing things. Earthly flowers, although living, make no immediate personal response when one comes into close touch with them. But here it is vastly different.

Spirit flowers are imperishable, and that should at once suggest more than mere life within them, and spirit flowers, as well as all other forms of nature, are created by the Great Father of the Universe through his agents in the realms of spirit. They are part of the immense stream of life that flows directly from Him, and that flows through every species of botanic growth. That stream never ceases, never falters, and it is, moreover, continuously fed by the admiration and love which we, in this world of spirit, gratefully shed upon such choice gifts of the Father.

Is it, then, to be wondered at, when we take the tiniest blossom within our hands, that we should feel such an influx of magnetic power, such a revivifying force, such an upliftment of one's very being, when we know, in truth, that those forces for our betterment are coming directly from the Source of all good? No, there is no other meaning behind our spirit flowers than the expressed beauty of the Father of the Universe, and, surely, that is enough. He has attached no strange symbolism to His faultless creations. Why should we?

## The Message of the Gifts

These are just some of the beautiful gifts of the spirit world. There are many more, described by scores of writers and mediums. It is certainly true that currently, the science of the physical world offers no proof of the reality of the spirit world or its beautiful gifts. However, the purpose of this essay is not to prove that they exist but to provide food for thought to those individuals who are open to the idea that the spirit world is indeed our final destination.

When I reflect about these gifts, I always come back to the same conclusion: that the Creator of the beautiful gifts of the spirit world must have been motivated by an intense and enduring love for each of us. Each of the gifts is so absolutely *perfect* for human beings—so fulfilling, so charming, and so delightful in every way. Each of the gifts fosters and multiplies love and beauty and joy. I believe that the realm of the spirit world was created to be a place of happiness that is almost unimaginable from our vantage point in the physical world, which has so often been described as "hell on earth."

To me, the message of the gifts of the spirit world is that the happiness of humans is entirely dependent upon our response to the call of love and beauty. As we work to resonate with love and beauty in our lives on earth, we will simultaneously create an expanding spiritual atmosphere all around us that will one day become the foundation of our home in the spirit world. An eternal world of love and beauty is available to all of us, without exception, and that, to me, is the most beautiful gift of all.

I love you. Let that really sink in. The God who created the universe loves *you*. What could be more comforting than that?

Stay with me. Rest in my embrace. Grow strong in my embrace. Become a vibrant being in my embrace. Grow and mature and become a purveyor of unconditional love in my embrace. My love and my embrace will lead you and guide you and strengthen you. The more you love me in return, the more you'll find the strength to love all those around you.

# About the Author

It's common for "About the Author" sections to be short bits of prose written in the third person. I've never seen one that included photos, as this one does. I've decided to break the rules and not only include photos but also write this section in the first person, and write more than a little snippet.

Although David Copperfield began his story with the chapter heading "I Am Born," I shall refrain from telling you that I was born under a canoe on Miami Beach while the moon gazed sympathetically at my mother as she was pelted with coconuts by monkeys howling in the palm trees.

I cannot say that my birth happened that way, for it did not, since I was instead born in a hospital in Coral Gables, Florida, in 1954, two months premature. It was quite unexciting but not dull, at least from my mother's point of view.

My mother, Polly Kapteyn Brown, was my best friend throughout my childhood. Although she was not a "huggy" type of person, she was someone whom I could trust and love and respect.

I arrived in life in the footsteps of my ancestors, starting with my parents. I owe them a profound debt for the goodness and merit that they left behind. In particular, my mother believed in my potential and gave me the vision, while I was young, to try to think on a grand philosophical scale. (I am still attempting to do that.) Polly was an artist and art teacher, first at the Portland School of Fine and Applied Arts (the precursor to MECA, the Maine College of Art), and then at a school called "Concept" that she founded with some fellow artists, including the noted Maine artist Bill Manning. In 1982, a year before she died from lung cancer, she earned a graduate degree from the Episcopal Divinity School in Cambridge, Massachusetts.

She was also a writer, poet, and philosopher, perhaps inspired by her aunt, and my grandaunt, Olga Fröbe-Kapteyn, a Dutch spiritualist, theosophist, and scholar. Olga was the founder of the Eranos Foundation in Ascona, Switzerland, and was a friend of Carl Gustav Jung's.

Olga was, in turn, inspired by her mother and my great-grandmother, Geertruida Agneta Kapteyn-Muysken, a humanist and leading social activist in nineteenth-century London. She was influenced by the French poet and philosopher Jean-Marie Guyau and counted George Bernard Shaw and Prince Pyotr Alexeyevich Kropotkin among her large circle of friends. She was an influential writer in London for twenty years and then moved to Zurich, where she became the center of a group of artists and students. Many Polish and Russian student émigrés regarded her as their "spiritual mother."[1]

This lineage of writers was unknown to me when I was a student. I believed that it was from my mother alone that I had inherited my passion for writing. I was thus quite fascinated when I learned more about the lives of Olga and Geertruida.

---

1. MUYSKEN, Geertruida Agneta. BWSA - Biografisch Woordenboek van het. Socialisme en de Arbeidersbeweging in Nederland.
https://socialhistory.org/bwsa/biografie/muysken
Web page viewed on December 10, 2016

## About the Author

My confidence to follow a writing career was also bolstered in my high school days, when my senior-class English teacher at the Waynflete School in Portland, the late William Ackley, said to me, "Brownie, you've got it. Keep going!" (Or something to that effect.) I kept going and am immensely grateful for his encouragement.

I am indeed fortunate to have met and married a wonderful lady who is also a writer and spiritualist, my dear bride, Kimmy Sophia. I affectionately call her "the Forest Queen." For many years, we co-published *The Significato Journal*, an online magazine with the theme "nectar for the soul" that emphasized the arts, nature, spirituality, and service. That magazine closed in 2020. The content has been moved to our respective websites (peterfalkenbergbrown.com and kimmysophiabrown.com ). We reside in my home state of Maine and have four grown children.

My father, Carl Falkenberg Brown, was the son of Norman Brown of Portland, Maine, and the Baroness Helen Dean Falkenberg, of Quebec City. "Granny" and her four siblings each inherited their titles from their father, Baron Fredrick Andreas Falkenberg, since their family received the title in 1733, starting with my fifth great-grandfather Gabriel Henriksson Falkenberg of Trystorp, Sweden, and thus by Swedish law did not follow the tradition of primogeniture.

Baron Gabriel married Countess Beata Margareta Douglas and was the grandson of Cunradt von Falkenberg, born in 1591.

My second great-grandfather Baron Gerhard Knut Alfrid Falkenberg was appointed Consul General to British North America in the 1800s and thus moved to Quebec, where eventually, my grandfather Norman met Baroness Helen and brought her back to Portland, Maine.

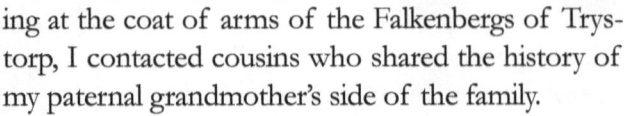

Since I have a great love of history and grew up looking at the coat of arms of the Falkenbergs of Trystorp, I contacted cousins who shared the history of my paternal grandmother's side of the family.

On the Brown side, Carl was the great-grandson of William Wentworth Brown, who purchased and developed what was to become the Brown Company in Berlin, New Hampshire. Second great-grandfather William (known as "W.W.") was the son of a farmer, Jonathan, born in 1776 in Hallowell, Maine.

Jonathan was a devout Christian and held Bible studies in the family home in Clinton, Maine, for forty years. Jonathan's lineage started in America with the arrival in Boston of my seventh great-grandfather William Browne, where he married my seventh great-grandmother Elizabeth Ruggles in 1655.

It is possible that William came from Dunfermline, Scotland, and may have emigrated to America to avoid Oliver Cromwell's armies, which would be ironic, considering that my seventh great-granduncle on my grandmother's side was the ruthless and infamous Charles Fleetwood, commander in chief of Cromwell's armies.

William Wentworth Brown built a logging and paper company that thrived for almost seventy years until the Great Depression and off-shore competition ended its run. At its height, the Brown Company owned four million acres of timberland and had turned tiny Berlin into a thriving town.

W.W. and his sons built a company known for its honesty and its kindness to its employees and the residents of Berlin. Although the family was unable to surmount the challenges of the Depression, a family historian wrote that when they failed, they "failed honorably."

By the time I was born, the Brown money was long gone, leaving my father to struggle and scrape and do his best to raise three children. Since we were poor, our family often returned to live in Granny's house, a large brick manse at 135 Vaughan Street in Portland's prosperous West End. Of all the many places I lived as a child, my grandmother's house was the one that I counted as home.

I've often reflected that growing up "poor" might have been for the best, since who knows what kind of person I would have been if I had been raised in wealth? Life is full of mysteries like that, but I am grateful that many of the wealthy Browns believed in kindness and honesty and

honor. To my mother, most especially, I am thankful that I inherited a deep love for writing and art and nature and music and all things of beauty. I've discovered that being surrounded by those gifts throughout my life gave me the experiential knowledge that I was the very opposite of poor.

I inherited an adventurous spirit from my ancestors. When I was eighteen, in 1973, I rode off into the sunset on a bicycle, headed for Mardi Gras in New Orleans, and then on to California. I spent two weeks traveling through the back roads of New England until I arrived at the Connecticut-New York border. Much to my surprise, after visiting my paternal aunt in New York City, I decided to stay and live in Manhattan.

My bicycle trip had been contemplative and had heightened my sense that I was on a spiritual search. I had kept a picture of Jesus next to my bed since I was four years old and had been inspired by books like *The Robe* by Lloyd C. Douglas, about a Roman soldier who gambled for Jesus' robe, converted to Christianity, and then died a martyr under Roman arrows. I had a strong desire to follow Jesus and wished that I could have been alive when he preached in Israel. My mother had also introduced me to other religious avenues, and as I arrived in New York in my quest to "go west, young man," I was busily reading books by Erich Fromm, J. Krishnamurti, and various Sufi authors.

I stayed in New York for a couple of years and then began a long process of exploring the rest of the country. Along the way, I became a writer, a web database programmer, and the Director of Web Operations for a magazine publishing company in New York City. After thirty-four years of gallivanting, I arrived back in Maine in 2007 with a wife, four children, two dogs, and a cat. A lot happens when you ride away into the sunset.

For many years now, I've been exploring a path that has a great similarity to the one followed by my philosopher mother. I've read many of the same ancient Christian mystics that she studied in her religious quest as an Episcopalian. As I delved into the writings of a broad range of mystics, I discovered what was to become one of my core beliefs—that no one can be closer to a person than the indwelling God. I can say with immense gratitude that I am passionately in love with God.

Partly through my own experience with God, I have developed a profound appreciation for the kind, gentle, compassionate, egalitarian, and respectful love that I feel that God has for each individual.

God is my Great Solace and my Best Friend. Deepening my awareness of God's presence and expressing God's love to others are the central goals of my life, both here and in my future life in the spirit world. I am grateful that my faith in God and my vision about a world of love have been profoundly informed by the mystics who taught about the indwelling God.

My life now is a tremendously exciting adventure—the mystical search to become resonant with the indwelling God of love and kindness and compassion.

It is a search imbued with daily enthusiasm and joy and the conviction that, as Deepak Chopra wrote in *How to Know God: The Soul's Journey into the Mystery of Mysteries*:

God enfolds the whole creation, not just the nice parts.

❧

At Two Lights, Cape Elizabeth, Maine

# Image Credits

Color images used inside the book have been converted to grayscale and some images (including the cover) have been cropped or modified.

## Cover Image

"The Soul of the Rose"
by John William Waterhouse, 1908
Oil on canvas, Width: 59.1 cm (23.2 in), Height: 88.3 cm (34.7 in)
Private Collection, By courtesy of Julian Hartnoll/Bridgeman Images
Back cover is a cropped and enlarged rectangle from the painting.

Cover design by the World Community Press and Great Northern Tea

**Images from the essay:**

**"Is There a God, and What is God Like?
Exploring the Evidence of Love"**

Photo of Viggo the Cat, by Peter Falkenberg Brown

Photo of the Crescent Beach Meadow, by Peter Falkenberg Brown

Image of Atom by Gerd Altmann, Public Domain

Painting of "God the Father and Angel," 1620
by Guercino (Giovan Francesco Barbieri), Public Domain

Painting of "An Angel Leading a Soul into Hell," 16th Century
by a follower of Hieronymus Bosch, Public Domain
Wellcome Library, London. Wellcome Images

Photo of Polly Kapteyn Brown, circa 1970, at Concept Art School, Portland, Maine. Photographer unknown

Photo of Shark, Fallows C, Gallagher AJ, Hammerschlag N (2013) Published in a Public Library of Science journal., CC BY 2.5

Photo of a 16-week old Kooikerhondje puppy, 2017 by Harriet Bedell-Pearce, CC BY-SA 4.0

Photo of a Carl F. Bucherer manufactured watch movement, 2016 by Carl F. Bucherer, CC BY-SA 2.0

Photo of Cover of Play: Romeo and Juliet, Public Domain

Painting of the famous balcony scene from Romeo and Juliet, 1884 Frank Dicksee (1853–1928), Public Domain

Photo of a chimpanzee seated at a typewriter, circa 1906 New York Zoological Society, Public Domain

Photo of LG G6, LG전자, CC BY 2.0

Photo of Honda NSX, User: Ed g2s, CC BY-SA 3.0

Photo of Air France Concorde, 2003, by Alexander Jonsson GNU Free Documentation License, Version 1.2

Photo of Laptop by AVADirect Custom Computers, 2015, Cmccarthy8 Creative Commons Attribution-Share Alike 4.0 International

Photo of neon theatre marquee, 2016, Jedi94 GNU Free Documentation License, Version 1.2

Video of Flamingos in the zoo of Wuppertal, 2013, by Frank Vincentz GNU Free Documentation License, Version 1.2

Image of Timeline showing different events in the evolution of life, 2012, LadyofHats, Creative Commons CC0 1.0 Universal Public Domain Dedication

Photo of Antony Flew, Public Domain

Image of Human DNA, double helix shape, 2016 by Pixabay, Creative Commons CC0 1.0 Universal Public Domain Dedication

Painting of "Never Morning Wore to Evening, but Some Heart Did Break," 1894, by Walter Langley, w1524 x h1220 mm, Public Domain

Painting of "The drowned fisherman," 1896 by Michael Peter Ancher, 289 × 212.5 cm, (Without frame) Statens Museum for Kunst, Public Domain

Image Credits

Photo of the Antennae Galaxies, 2013
The NASA/ESA Hubble Space Telescope, ESA/Hubble & NASA, (CC BY 4.0)

Photo of Chipmunk (Tamias striatus) taken at Garret Mountain,
West Paterson, NJ, Photographer: Magnus Manske, (CC BY-SA 2.0)

Photo of Anatolian Shepherd guarding his flock, 2012
by Sirswindon, GNU Free Documentation License, Version 1.2

Photo of A dramatic sunset, 2005
Fir0002 at en.wikipedia, GNU Free Documentation License, Version 1.2

Image of positions and names of planets in the Solar System, 2013, by WP
Creative Commons Attribution-Share Alike 3.0 Unported

Photo of Contemporary ballet, 2005, by Jeff from Denver, US
Creative Commons Attribution-Share Alike 2.0 Generic

Painting of "The Creation of Adam," circa 1511
by Michelangelo di Lodovico Buonarroti Simoni, Public Domain

Photo of Giraffa camelopardalis reticulata, 2007
Brookenovak, Creative Commons Attribution 2.0 Generic

Photo of Flowers (Blooms53), 2013
by Korona Lacasse, Creative Commons Attribution 2.0 Generic

Photo of A baby wearing many items of winter clothing, 2007
by Andrew Vargas from Clovis, United States
Creative Commons Attribution 2.0 Generic

Painting of "Berceuse (Le coucher)" [Lullaby (Bedtime)], 1873
by William-Adolphe Bouguereau
Oil on canvas, 112 x 86.5 cm (3 ft. 8 in. x 2 ft. 10 in.)
Image courtesy of the Art Renewal Center
www.artrenewalcenter.org

Painting of "Chained Prisoner," between 1806 and 1812
by Francisco de Goya, Indian ink wash
Height: 218 mm (8.58 in). Width: 151 mm (5.94 in), Public Domain

Photo of Deinotherium (German: Hauerelefant), 2008
Museum am Löwentor, Stuttgart, by Ra'ike
GNU Free Documentation License, Version 1.2

Painting of "A Soul Carried to Heaven"
by William-Adolphe Bouguereau, Public Domain

Most Images from Wikimedia Commons

## About the Author

Photo of author speaking, from video shot by author

Photo of Polly Kapteyn Brown, photographer unknown

Photo of Olga Fröbe-Kapteyn at Eranos in the 1940s.
Photograph by Margarethe Fellerer, Eranos Foundation Archives
Used with permission of the Fondazione Eranos, Ascona, Switzerland

Photo of Geertruida Agneta Kapteyn-Muysken
Public Domain. G.A. Muysken, Internationaal Archief
voor de Vrouwenbeweging (Amsterdam).
Originally published in *BWSA* 2 (1987), p. 95-97.
https://socialhistory.org/bwsa/biografie/muysken.

Photo of Kimmy Sophia Brown, Botanical Gardens, by the author

Photo of Carl Falkenberg Brown, photographer unknown

Photo of Norman Brown and Baroness Helen Dean Falkenberg Brown, photographer unknown

Painting of Baron Gabriel Henriksson Falkenberg of Trystorp, Sweden
Oil on canvas, 144x114 cm, by Lorens Pasch the Elder. Date unknown. Cropped.

Painting of Countess Beata Margareta Douglas, oil on canvas, 78x64 cm.
by Lorens Pasch the Elder. Date unknown. Painting is cropped.

Painting of Cunradt von Falkenberg. Oil on canvas, 192x105 cm.
by Jacob Heinrich Elbfas. Date unknown. Painting is cropped.

Photo (cropped) of Baron Gerhard Knut Alfrid Falkenberg, by Johannes Jaeger.

Painting of Falkenberg of Trystorp Coat of Arms, by Jan Raneke, 1982

Photo of Jonathan Brown, photographer unknown

Painting of William Wentworth Brown
by Frederick Porter Vinton, Boston, MA, USA
Painted in 1902, oil on canvas, 4' x 5' (framed), commissioned for $1,600.
Used with permission of the Brown Memorial Library, Clinton, ME.

Photos of family at Vaughan Street, Portland, ME, photographer unknown

Photo of author on bicycle at Vaughan Street, Portland, ME, by family member

Photo of author at Crescent Beach, Cape Elizabeth ME, by James Brown

Photo of author at Two Lights, Cape Elizabeth, ME, by Kimmy Sophia Brown

www.ingramcontent.com/pod-product-compliance
Lightning Source LLC
Chambersburg PA
CBHW032026290426
44110CB00012B/696